Warman's®
Vintage Quilts

IDENTIFICATION AND PRICE GUIDE

Published by

kp krause publications
An Imprint of F+W Publications

700 East State Street • Iola, WI 54990-0001
715-445-2214 • 888-457-2873
www.krausebooks.com

Our toll-free number to place an order or obtain
a free catalog is (800) 258-0929.

Library of Congress Control Number: 2008928412

ISBN-13: 978-089689-687-1
ISBN-10: 0-89689-687-0

Designed by Katrina Newby
Edited by Joe Kertzman

Printed in China

Warman's
Vintage Quilts

IDENTIFICATION AND PRICE GUIDE

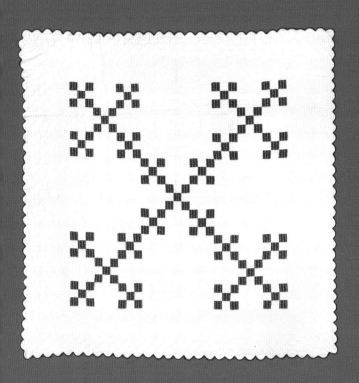

Maggi McCormick Gordon

More Great Books in the Warman's® Series

Warman's® Antiques & Collectibles Price Guide
Warman's® Carnival Glass
Warman's® Children's Books
Warman's® Civil War Collectibles
Warman's® Civil War Weapons
Warman's® Coca-Cola Collectibles®
Warman's® Coins and Paper Money
Warman's® Cookie Jars
Warman's® Costume Jewelry Figurals
Warman's® Depression Glass
Warman's® Dolls: Antique to Modern
Warman's® Duck Decoys
Warman's® English & Continental Pottery & Porcelain
Warman's® Fenton Glass
Warman's® Fiesta Ware
Warman's® Flea Market Price Guide
Warman's® Gas Station Collectibles
Warman's® Hull Pottery
Warman's® Jewelry
Warman's® Little Golden Books
Warman's® Majolica
Warman's® McCoy Pottery
Warman's® North American Indian Artifacts
Warman's® Political Collectibles
Warman's® Red Wing Pottery
Warman's® Rookwood Pottery
Warman's® Roseville Pottery
Warman's® Sporting Collectibles
Warman's® Sterling Silver Flatware
Warman's® Vietnam War Collectibles
Warman's® Vintage Jewelry
Warman's® Weller Pottery
Warman's® World War II Collectibles

Warman's® Companion series
Carnival Glass
Collectible Dolls
Depression Glass
Fenton Glass
Fiesta
Hallmark Keepsake Ornaments
Hot Wheels
McCoy Pottery
PEZ®
Roseville Pottery
U.S. Coins & Currency
Watches
World Coins & Currency

CONTENTS

TABLE OF CONTENTS

Introduction | 6
How to use this guide | 6
Chapter 1: Starting A Collection | 7
Where to look | 7
Where to purchase | 7
Dealers, auction houses, retail outlets, eBay and other online sites | 9
Understanding quilts | 9
Detecting fakes and repairs | 10
Understanding the marketplace | 12
Buying antique quilts | 12
Condition and workmanship | 12
Dating quilts | 14
Fabrics, patterns, technique, the four B's, quilting, colors and dyes | 14
Getting an appraisal | 17
Insuring your quilts | 17
Keeping a collection | 18
Repair or finish? | 18
Cleaning | 18
Storaging your quilt | 18
Displaying your quilts | 19
Enjoying your quilts | 21

Chapter 2: Patchwork Quilts | 22
Wholecloth, Strippies and Frames | 24
Strips and Strings | 34
Log Cabin | 40
One-Patch | 55
Traditional Blocks | 71
Representational Blocks | 112
Signatures | 141
Curves | 147
Chapter 3: Appliqué | 160
Sunbonnet Sue | 162
Pictorials and Florals 164
Chapter 4: Embellished Quilts | 184
Embroidered Quilts | 185
Crazy Quilts | 191
Chapter 5: Small Quilts | 198
Crib Quilts | 199
Doll Quilts | 221
Chapter 6: Non-traditional Quilts | 234
African-American | 235
Siddi | 248

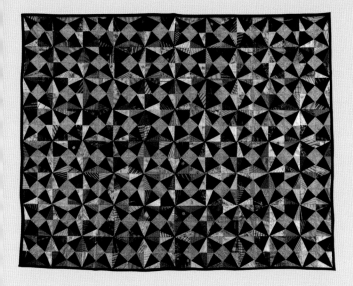

Introduction: How to Use This Guide

While not all quilters collect quilts, and not all quilt collectors are quilters, there is nevertheless a crossover between the two interests. Collectors collect quilts for many reasons. A collection can begin with family heirlooms. Perhaps your great-grandmother made quilts and taught your grandmother. She taught your mother, and then your mother taught you (though if you are a child of the late 20th century, you may have learned quilting skills in other ways).

Each generation made quilts, comforters and coverlets, all intended to be used. Many were used into oblivion and rest in quilt heaven, but for myriad reasons, some have survived. Many of them remain because they were not used but stored, often forgotten, in trunks and linen cabinets.

Perhaps they didn't suit the new color scheme in your parents' home. When your parents downsized, you discovered a treasure trove that sparked your interest, and now you are adding to the family collection.

Sometimes a quilt just catches your eye. Though I had a few quilts before, my own collecting really began with a red-and-white strippy quilt from the Northeast of England spotted in an antiques store in Edinburgh, Scotland. Though it was made probably in the 1880s, its graphic qualities were so modern that it stopped my husband and me in our tracks and we had to have it. We haven't stopped collecting since.

Some people begin with a quilt to match a new home decorating scheme. Others are given a quilt as a gift. Some are interested in quilts as historical documents, and still others see them as art. All these reasons are valid, and there are probably almost as many reasons as there are collectors.

This book is intended to help you find your way through the enormous variety of quilts that are available on the open market. All of the quilts featured are in private hands. Some are beautiful, elaborate, elegant examples of museum quality. Others are faded, even worn in places, but are representative of the sorts of quilts that can be found in flea markets, secondhand outlets, antiques stores, auction galleries, and of course on eBay.

One of the quilts shown was retrieved by its owner from a dumpster. Its offbeat color scheme might not appeal to everyone, but she liked what she found after she'd washed it, and it makes a great story, especially when told in front of her son who was with her when she climbed into the dumpster to fetch it. He is embarrassed to this day. Another of the generous collectors represented describes herself with a laugh as a "humane society for quilts."

Among the quilts shown are those made across the United States and a few from England, almost all pre-1950s. They may have been chosen because they represent a type of quilt that has deep roots in the society from which they came. Some are unusual variations of traditional patterns, while others are beautiful examples of color combining. Each one is unique, and all demonstrate artistic merit, whether the maker considered herself an artist or not.

The quilts are divided into five main categories: Pieced (also known as patchwork) quilts, Appliqué quilts, Embellished quilts, Small quilts, and Non-traditional quilts. The section on Small quilts is divided into crib and doll versions. The final category contains examples that are late 20th century, but are areas that are considered highly collectible. Within the five main headings, you will find quilts, comforters, coverlets and unfinished tops that fall into the category.

Within each section the quilts are divided by pattern or style. Wherever possible, particular color combinations are shown together. I hope the arrangement will make it easy to use this guide, since some collectors focus on quilts from a certain time period, or buy only quilts of a particular color combination, such as red and white or blue and white. Others specialize in appliquéd or embroidered quilts, while some collect small quilts. I hope this arrangement will make it straightforward for each collector to use the guide effectively and efficiently.

Each featured quilt has an informational caption containing the facts that are known about the piece: the kind of quilt it is, the date as far as can be determined, the maker and geographical area if known, a description of the quilt, and the price range.

CHAPTER 1

STARTING A COLLECTION

Where to look

If you inherited or were given a quilt or a few, you were perhaps intrigued into wanting to know more. The subject of quilts is vast, and lifetimes have been spent in studying the history of these fascinating textile artifacts. As with most collecting, quilts can become an obsession, and for many of us the more we know, the more we want to know, and the more we feel we can never know enough. Looking at quilts is, I think, the best way to learn about what to look for when you are thinking of purchasing, but reading books—about the history, the techniques, the fabrics, the dyes—is also valuable.

Go to exhibitions in museums, galleries and historical societies. Public institutions with quilt collections seldom display more than a few of their pieces at any one time, but many will open their vaults to serious researchers. Contact the curator in charge to try to arrange access, but don't expect to be able to touch most of the quilts, even when wearing white gloves. Attend viewings at auction houses and go to estate sales. Look in consignment houses, secondhand and thrift shops, and flea markets. Talk to other collectors and dealers, who are usually willing and eager to share their knowledge and expertise, and to let you look closely and handle their wares.

Research the history of any type of quilt that particularly interests you. The more you know, the more savvy you become as a collector. The American attitude toward quilts is romantic, but quilts are much more than idealized objects. These textiles are part of our history and culture. They are documents that tell stories if we know how to read them. The early colonists brought quilts with them,

In this chapter
7 Where to look
7 Where to purchase
9 Understanding quilts
12 Buying antique quilts
18 Keeping a collection
21 Enjoying your collection

and quilts were made in pre-Revolutionary times. The westward-bound pioneers took with them quilts made in their original homes, often by family and friends as farewell gifts, and they made more as they headed into the vast middle of the country.

Events such as the Centennial Exposition of 1876 in Philadelphia and the 1933 Chicago "Century of Progress" World's Fair altered the direction of quiltmaking. Finding out about the techniques used to make quilts and the reasons, technological and cultural, as to how and why changes in fashion and method happened, will help you make informed decisions about whether or not a quilt is a smart acquisition, one that adds value and depth to your collection.

There are magazines devoted to quilts, and though none of them is aimed primarily at the collector, several have interesting articles about the history of quilts and quiltmaking from time to time. Magazines and newsletters from large collecting institutions that have quilts as part of their collections sometimes publish articles, particularly connected to upcoming exhibitions. The Internet is increasingly worthwhile for anyone doing research about vintage quilts. Type in "vintage quilts" and Google's search engine will give you 355,000 options; try "history of quilts" to get 285,000. Many will be repeats, but it's a good way to start.

Where to purchase

Once upon a time (and this is not a fairy tale), it was possible to go, particularly into rural areas around the United States, and happen upon vintage quilts of astonishing variety and quality that were being sold for a song. Even today, when most people seem to have cottoned onto the inherent value of quilts, avid collectors still sometimes spot

a treasure being used in an unconventional, and usually inappropriate, way, like the one being used to wrap the picnic gear at a tailgate party before a baseball game. The friends who were with the quilt lover who spotted it pooled their cash to lend to her, and she bought a blue and white quilt for $75 on the spot. These stories are, sadly for the frugal collector, less common than they used to be, although there were hundreds of thousands of quilts made over the past two centuries, and many beautiful ones still turn up in attics and trunks. Many of the best examples are now in museum collections, and rightly so, and others are with dealers who picked them up at estate sales or auctions.

Dealers

Dealers' markups can be substantial, but generally they know their stock and price accordingly. Quality is usually high, and most dealers also have interesting but less unusual quilts that carry affordable price tags. There are plenty of dealers who have no premises to maintain who scour the country looking for stock, which they then sell at shows and fairs, or from their homes or on the Internet. Dealers are often open to negotiation, especially if you are buying more than one quilt. Many will allow you to take a quilt on approval, particularly if you have established a relationship with them.

Auction houses

Interestingly, reasonably priced vintage quilts can be purchased at one of the many auctions held around the country every year. Every major metropolitan area in the country has a few auction houses, each with its website. Many of these establishments hold sales of textiles, including quilts, from time to time. Check online for upcoming sales, where most of the items will be pictured and described. However, try to attend a viewing session if you see anything you are interested in, because looking at thumbnails is completely different from seeing, and handling, the real thing.

Auction purchases cannot be returned, and there is no substitute for beholding with your own eyes. Many houses have an expert or appraiser on whom they rely for help with pricing, dating, etc., but few have an in-house curator who specializes in quilts, so the more knowledge you have, the better placed you are to spot a treasure.

Most auctions are live events, with potential buyers seated in the room. Many have telephone hook-ups and increasingly allow bidding by Internet, as well. Purchasers sitting in the auction room register their details and are given a numbered paddle. The auctioneer names a starting bid, and if you wish to bid on an item, you hold up the paddle. If a higher bid is then made, the auctioneer will come back to you to see if you want to increase your bid,

and bidding stops when no one makes a higher offer.

Telephone bidders speak in real time to a member of the auction house staff who relays your bid to the auctioneer, and Internet bidders relay their offers online. Bidding at auction may seem daunting, and there's no question that it can get the adrenaline going, but it is a great way to pick up bargains.

A word of warning about bidding out of house: It is easy to get carried away, and it can be difficult to judge what's happening if you are not in the room. However, some auction companies have embraced technology wholeheartedly by conducting their sales entirely online through their websites, although the increasing use of web cams will no doubt give bidders a better feel for the situation in a live setting.

One reason for buying at auction is that prices can be lower than they are in an antiques store or from a dealer. However, there is usually a premium charged by the auction house, an extra charge of about 10 percent to help cover its costs. If you are not in a position to take the goods with you at the end of the sale—and you must pay all the charges before the quilts are handed over—you will also incur shipping charges. You will also be responsible for any storage fees that the auctioneer charges for goods left for more than a specified period of time, usually about a week, which give payments and checks time to clear. Online bidding is usually subject to the same rules and fees.

Of course, you can also sell at auction if you wish to de-accession part or all of a collection. Auctioning a collection can attract attention, which probably increases the number of potential buyers, but bear in mind that the auction house deducts a percentage of the price of each sale, generally about 25 percent.

Other retail outlets

Other places to look for vintage quilts include estate sales and general antiques stores. The outcomes will be very hit-or-miss, but if you enjoy the search and have the time, you may find the occasional treasure at a bargain price. Consignment houses, secondhand stores, resale shops, and flea markets are also worth a visit. You will be able to examine potential purchases in all of these places. Look carefully at condition and avoid getting carried away by a price that seems cheap, only to get it home and discover that it is falling apart.

eBay and other online sites

Purchasing online has become a way of life, and eBay is by far the largest outlet for quilts or practically anything else. Bidding online at live auctions (see above) is one way to buy quilts, but prices on eBay are generally hard to match. To bid online, you must register before you can place a bid. Items generally are pictured with a few detail shots included, plus information about the piece. I have found that listed items sometimes carry inaccurate information, such as the wrong name for the pattern or a date that is out of line. This is, I suspect, more often ignorance of the subject on the part of the seller, who provides the information, than willful misinformation.

Someone who inherits the trunk in Grandma's attic, that turns out to be filled with quilts that he or she has no room or use for, may not have access to expert information. You can contact the seller by email through the site to ask questions, and each item has a feedback box that includes an evaluation of the seller's past transactions.

Bids are timed, or you can "buy it now" if you want to place the maximum bid. Placing a bid constitutes a binding contract, should your bid be the highest. You then must pay for the item online, using PayPal, and the item will be shipped to you. Shipping charges are listed next to the price of the item. The site will request feedback, and your transaction is complete.

It can be difficult to return items unless they are vastly different from the description, so contact the seller in advance if you have any qualms about what you might be buying, and confirm that you can return it if it is not what you thought. Remember that the stock changes continually, so it is worth keeping an eye on the screen, but bear in mind that it is also easy to get carried away, so set limits for yourself. Don't forget to use the Internet to research the type of quilt you are looking at to get as much information as possible before you buy.

Understanding Quilts

This book is not the place for a long history of quilt-making, but a bit of background information will be useful. A quilt is a very specific being. Technically, a quilt is made up of three layers: a top, which can be a solid piece of fabric, appliquéd, pieced or a combination; the back, which can be another solid piece of fabric, or pieced; and the batting, which is the center layer that can be cotton, wool, polyester, a blend of poly and cotton, or even silk.

Many vintage quilts are batted with an old blanket or even an old, worn quilt. The fabrics are usually cotton or wool, or fine fancy fabrics like silk, velvet, satin and taffeta. The layers of a true quilt are held together by the stitching, or quilting, that goes through all three layers and is usually worked in a design or pattern that enhances the piece overall. The term "quilt" has become synonymous with bedcover to many people, and we include tied quilts, comforters and quilt tops, none of which are true quilts in the technical description, in this book.

Quilts made from a seemingly single solid piece of fabric are known as *wholecloth quilts*, or if they are white, as *whitework* quilts. Usually such quilts are constructed from two or more pieces of the same fabric joined to make up the necessary width. They are often quilted quite elaborately, and the seams virtually disappear within the decorative stitching. Most wholecloth quilts are solid-colored, but prints were also used. Whitework quilts were often made as bridal quilts and many were kept for "best," which means that they have survived in reasonable numbers.

Wholecloth quilts were among the earliest type of quilted bedcovers made in Britain, and the colonists brought examples with them according to inventory lists that exist from colonial times. American quiltmakers used the patterns early in the nation's history, and some were carried with settlers moving west across the Appalachians.

Appliqué quilts are made from shapes cut from fabric and applied, or appliquéd, to a background, usually solid-colored on vintage quilts, to make a design. Early appliqué quilts dating back to the 18th century were often worked in a technique called *broderie perse*, or Persian embroidery, in which printed motifs were cut from a piece of fabric, such as costly chintz, and applied to a plain, less expensive background cloth.

Appliqué was popular in the 1800s, and there are thousands of examples, from exquisite, brightly colored Baltimore Album quilts made in and around Baltimore between circa 1840 and 1860, to elegant four-block quilts made later in the century. Many appliqué quilts are pictorial—with floral designs the predominant motif. In the 20th century, appliqué again enjoyed an upswing, especially during the Colonial Revival period, and thousands were made from patterns or the mainly appliqué kits that were marketed and sold from 1900 through the 1950s.

Pieced, or patchwork, quilts are made by cutting fabric into shapes and sewing them together to make a larger piece of cloth. The patterns are usually geometric, and their effectiveness depends heavily on the contrast of not just the colors themselves, but of color value as well. Patchwork became popular in the United States in the early 1800s.

Colonial clothing was almost always made using cloth cut into squares or rectangles, but after the Revolutionary War, when fabric became more widely available, shaped garments were made that left scraps. Frugal housewives, especially among the westward-bound pioneers, began to use these cutoffs to put together blocks that could then be made into quilts. Patchwork quilts are by far the most numerous of all vintage-quilt categories, and the diversity of style, construction and effect that can be found is a study all its own.

Many collectors focus on one type of quilt, based on the technique perhaps, or within a color range or a particular time period. Others are entranced by variety and assemble highly eclectic collections covering many areas of the quiltmaker's art. A study of any aspect of the subject that interests you will pay dividends as you add items to your own collection.

Detecting fakes and repairs

Sadly, as in most areas of collecting, the unscrupulous exist and try to pass off quilts as being something that they are not. However, I believe that this happens less often than cases in which a dealer or private seller simply does not have the information they need to describe a quilt accu-

rately. Dating a quilt is always tricky, and it is here that the uninformed or unwary purchaser can be most easily misled.

One thing to look out for is the use of reproduction fabrics, which abound, and can fool even the eagle-eyed on occasion. Repro prints from the Civil War era and the 1930s are particularly popular, and while it can be hard to age new fabrics sufficiently to pass them off as being 150 years older than they are, it is possible. It is easier to deceive with the 1930s prints, especially if they are washed a few times, or if it is claimed that pieces are "unused" and "never laundered."

The Pinwheel variation quilt shown bottom left contains typical repro prints in a pattern that was made during the '30s and could be mistaken for an older piece. It was in fact made in 1999, but the maker has been careful to explain its origin and date fully on her label on the back.

Pay particular attention when buying a crib-sized quilt. There are countless quilts around that are categorized as "cutters." These are bed quilts that are stained or damaged too badly to retain much value, and quiltmakers and other crafters often cut out the usable parts and make them into pillows, stuffed toys, and smaller quilts. A true vintage crib quilt is usually more expensive inch for inch than all but the finest of bed quilts, and the unwary might be sold a cut-down piece at an inflated price.

The pattern on a crib quilt should be scaled smaller than it would be on a full-sized example. A frequent give-away to a cut-down is that it contains a few large blocks and has no border, such as the pink and white hearts quilt shown here, which was cut down by the owner, who tried

to repair the large quilt but found it was disintegrating in too many places to save. The other crib-size piece shown was cut down and is not yet finished. You may decide to purchase anyway if the price is right, but you should know what you are getting.

Another practice to watch for is the finishing of a vintage top. Many collectors purchase vintage tops in order to finish them, which means that they can be used and that they are stabilized for future generations to enjoy. Using age-appropriate vintage fabrics that provide the right visual balance to create borders, binding and backing means that the finished quilt will look vintage, but the seller should always tell a prospective buyer the history of the quilt. Remember that the quilting will not have been done by the original quiltmaker either.

Sets of vintage blocks that have never been assembled can also be found in large numbers, especially on Internet sites. Putting them together and finishing a quilt is another way of saving them for posterity, but again, purchasers should always be informed of the quilt's past.

The Fan quilt shown next was made from vintage fabrics that had been cut into the fan blades, and about 50 of the fans had been assembled. The collector who owned them added handles and backgrounds using vintage fabrics, and made the border from vintage feedsacks. A typical '30s quilt made in the 1990s, this owner has also labeled the piece so there is no mistaking its provenance.

Damaged quilts are often repaired by collectors who are also quiltmakers. If repairs are made skillfully with age-appropriate fabric, they can be virtually undetectable, but again, sellers should inform interested buyers of the facts. Well-made repairs can stabilize a quilt and give it a whole new lease on life, and in some cases may even enhance the value of the piece, but honesty is still the best policy.

Provenance can also be an issue. Many quilts were handed down through families with their stories told and retold for each new generation. Written documentation from original makers is usually hard to come by, however, and inaccuracies can occur in retelling the history of Great Aunt Sally's wedding quilt. Serving an internal pinch of salt with any purchase you are considering is an excellent idea.

Be particularly wary of any item that purports to be an "underground railroad" quilt. The romantic story of quilts being used to mark the safe houses and routes used by escaping slaves in the mid-1800s is disputed among scholars, and if such quilts existed, they would have turned up long ago. Many quilts made during the right timeframe, and even more since, are patterns that are claimed by the single source for the theory to be designs that were used, but until more evidence is found, this is an area to beware.

Understanding the marketplace

Collecting quilts is still a minority pastime. Other types of textiles such as embroidered samplers and woven coverlets bring higher prices, especially on the basis of the ratio of square inches to dollars. Knowing how to judge a good buy is a key to being a happy collector.

Determining the price for a quilt is a problem for everyone involved. Prices vary widely. Buyers in different areas of the country are interested in different types of quilts and in different patterns. Availability of certain designs or kinds of quilts can have an effect on the price, and the location of the seller might affect that aspect.

There are probably more Amish and Mennonite quilts in areas where these groups settled and more Baltimore Album quilts in and around Maryland than in other parts of the country. On the other hand, the number of kit quilts that appear on the market in some places may be related to the fact that there was a good local store selling them and offering advice and even instruction for quilters in their area.

Every locale has its own idea of the value of goods, and every potential buyer has a limit. To a great extent price is set by what a purchaser is willing to pay for a particular example and how long a seller wants to hold onto the merchandise. Learning as much as possible about the types of quilts you are interested in means that you are in a position to decide whether the piece is worth the asking price in the marketplace, as well as to you personally.

Current fashion also plays a part in setting prices. When minimalism became the style for home decor with the advent of urban loft conversions, Amish quilts with their bold color-field aesthetic became must-have items and prices skyrocketed. The still-undervalued African American market received a great boost from the traveling exhibit *The Quilts of Gee's Bend*. Log Cabin is a perennial favorite, but luckily there are probably tens of thousands of examples in circulation, so prices depend more on quality than this year's whim.

The more rare a particular quilt, in terms of its design, fabrics used or the quality of the quilting, for example, the higher the price is likely to be. Because many museum-quality quilts are now where they belong—in museums—those with outstanding and/or unique features in pristine condition are difficult to find, and if you should happen upon one, expect to see an outstanding price tag on it. There are, however, vast numbers of quilts that fall in a middle level between the extraordinary and the cutters.

Prices here are generally in the hundreds-to-low-thousands-of-dollars range, where most collectors find themselves as buyers. A few quilts have sold for more than $100,000 in recent years, but they are few and far between, and most have ended up in public collections.

Buying Antique Quilts

Condition and workmanship

Assessing the condition of a vintage quilt is not the only, or even the most important criterion for determining a fair value, but it is a good place to begin. A quilt in unused/unwashed/like new condition is rare these days, but they still turn up occasionally. Such an example is more valuable than a quilt of similar pattern and age that has been used and subjected to numerous washings. A more heavily used piece with an unusual design, great age or rare fabrics should not be overlooked. If a quilt has been cleaned or repaired for sale, the seller should tell the prospective purchaser.

Fading, which can be caused by cleaning, folding or exposure to light, is detrimental to value. Stains can sometimes be removed with proper cleaning, and generally cause less of a drop in value than fading. Holes in the fabric can be caused by moths or mice, or through human damage. People using the quilt more often than not create rips and tears, usually by accident.

Deterioration through aging, especially the shattering of some silks and satins, but also in fabrics colored with corrosive dyes, is another factor to look out for. Some of these flaws can be repaired or stabilized, but again purchasers should always be told if such work has been carried out. Quilts that have been stored badly often have fold lines that cannot be removed and may show some color loss.

Bindings are the first place where wear occurs on most quilts. If the quilt looks or feels old but the binding seems new, it probably is. The backing of original bindings on 19th-century quilts were turned to the front of the piece, or they were knife-edge, with the edges of the backing and the top turned toward the inside of the quilt to hide the batting, and stitched with running stitch close to the edge.

Quilts from the late 1800s were often bound separately, but if the binding fabric is original it will generally match the quilt fabrics in look and feel. If a seller has replaced a worn binding, it is unethical not to inform a prospective purchaser.

A pristine quilt, should you come across one, will look and feel different from one that has been used and washed. The fabrics will probably still have the sizing used to finish the cloth at the mill, and it will feel stiffer than material that has been washed. If it has been properly stored, it should not show fading or fold marks. Many unused quilts still show the markings for the quilting pattern, though the pencil markers favored by 19th-century makers were sometimes hard to remove even after several washings. Laundered fabrics will be smoother and softer than unwashed ones.

Cutters are quilts that are badly damaged or too heavily worn to be used as quilts. During the late 20th-century revival of quiltmaking, in the 1980s and '90s, many of the damaged quilts that turned up were cut up (or cut down) and made into everything from crib quilts and wall hangings to stuffed toys and bibs.

Crafters still carry out this practice, which has the merit of preserving patterns and fabrics of interest, but many cutter quilts are now sold as they are, which leaves buyers to decide what to do with the pieces. Some can be repaired, and quilt historians and textile experts use others for research purposes. Many collecting institutions, from dedicated quilt museums to textile conservation departments, will accept damaged quilts as donations, preferably without repairs that would affect the original look or intent of the makers.

Workmanship should also be considered in determining value. The most visible aspect of a vintage quilt is the quilting itself. Quilting was worked to hold the batting securely. Before the advent of commercially felted batts, cotton or wool fibers were laid on the quilt back and spread as evenly as possible to cover it. The top was then placed right side up to complete the quilt sandwich, and the layers were stitched together with quilting.

Unless the stitching was worked closely, the batting fibers shifted, creating lumps and bumps and migrating into corners. Rows tended to be worked about ¼-inch apart, and the quilter's aim was to make stitches that were both small and even. Small, even stitches are the most desirable on a traditional quilt, but utilitarian quilts and those made in the African-American tradition will be quilted with larger, often uneven stitches.

Bear in mind that utilitarian examples usually have a lower value in any case. Stitches are measured by the number of stitches in a 1-inch line, and the rule of thumb is that quilting that exceeds 10 stitches to the inch increases value. If stitches are of uneven length, value is affected downward.

The overall design of the quilting pattern is another important factor. Patchwork quilts with complex designs are generally quilted with simple line quilting, but wholecloth and appliquéd quilts often feature stunning patterns and motifs that add to their value, especially if the quilting is well executed.

The value of pieced quilts is affected by the characteristics involved in their assembly. The overall arrangement and the color balance help determine the uniqueness of a quilt, and the skill of the seamstress in putting the quilt together, whether by hand or machine, is of great importance. Corners where blocks or elements of blocks meet should be square, and points should be pointed, not cut off by the adjoining units.

Sashing should be level in both directions and blocks should be the same size unless a deliberate decision has been made to do otherwise. The setting of a quilt—the way the blocks are placed—can make the difference between a fascinating and even unique example and a mundane one.

Borders should enhance the quilt overall. A border is a frame for the main pattern and should be pleasing in proportion to the size of the blocks and the entire top, and in its colors. If borders are cut from print fabrics, they should be in keeping with print fabrics in the quilt.

Color choices are also important. One factor that contributes to an outstanding quilt is the contrast not just in the colors themselves, but also in the values—the perceived lightness or darkness—of the fabrics. High-contrast combinations are almost always more successful than using fabrics that are similar in value, provided the colors work well together. White or black combined with almost any other color is a successful, and widely used, pairing. Fabric scraps can be sorted into lights and darks, though value often depends on the colors adjacent to a particular piece. Scrap quilts that display excellent contrast are generally more desirable than those in which the differences are less obvious.

Well-made appliqué quilts are generally priced higher than pieced quilts from the same era, because they are more rare than the patchwork examples and because many of them have survived in near-pristine condition. Because appliqué is a time-consuming technique, examples made in the 19th and early 20th centuries were in many cases reserved by the household for "best" and received less wear and laundering than their pieced sisters.

Many of them also have elaborate quilting designs, and if they are beautifully worked, they will probably carry a high value. The stitching used to apply the pieces should be almost impossible to see without lifting the applied shape carefully, and there should be no frayed edges anywhere. Most of the kit quilts made in the first half of 1900s are appliqué, and the same rules apply to them.

The exception is on some appliqué quilts made between about 1865 and 1885 after the sewing machine became a fixture in many homes. In order to show off their technological marvel, many seamstresses used a machine topstitch to apply their shapes. Again, there should be no fraying, and the stitching should be even and well executed, with no lumps or burbles. Because of their age and relative rarity, well-made examples are high-value items.

Dating quilts

Dating a quilt is a tricky business unless the maker included the date on the finished item, and unfortunately for historians and collectors, few did. The notable exception is among Crazy Quilts, many of which, though far from all, are dated and signed. Knowing when a quilt was finished, which is the way in which quilt dates are assigned, is not always crucial to a decision to purchase, but most collectors like having as much information as possible. The value of a particular example is affected by its age, of course, and educating yourself about dating methods is invaluable. There are several aspects that can offer guidelines for establishing a date.

FABRICS

The first is usually to look at the fabrics in the quilt. Solid-colored fabrics are extremely difficult to date, and collectors need to know something about fabrics, dyes and colors in order to make reasonable assessments. Prints can offer more clues, and there are several books available to offer guidance.

Any quilt that includes synthetic fabrics is by necessity no older than the early 20th century, because before 1900 all cloth came from natural sources, i.e., cotton, wool, silk and linen. Rayon, introduced in the 1880s in Britain, and in the United States in 1910, is made from wood pulp or cot-

ton lint. It is therefore a natural fiber, but provides a dating clue. Synthetic polyester fibers were invented in the 1950s, so a quilt containing any of the many kinds or blends of polyesters were made after that.

There are several particular kinds of natural fabrics that can help in dating. One of the earliest is linsey-woolsey, woven with a wool weft and a linen warp. It has a rough finish and was used for everyday quilts in America, particularly during colonial times. Some people refer to whole-cloth quilts from the same period by the name linsey-woolsey if they have a linen top and a wool back.

Another early fabric used for late 18th- and early 19th-century quilts is calamanco, or *calimanco*. This is a wool cloth that has been hot-pressed to give it sheen. It was available in several jewel colors, and at first glance it looks something like silk, but it is heavy and scratchy. It was widely used in colonial households to make wholecloth quilts.

Early American quilters also used homespun, usually wool but occasionally cotton, particularly for backs, but home spinning was a dying skill even before the Civil War. Homespun in a quilt usually places it in the first half of the 1800s. Printed cotton chintz, usually unglazed, was available early in the 19th century, and many of the patterns are documented and dated, which provides the earliest possible date a quilt could have been made.

During the last quarter of the 19th century, various fabrics became popular with quiltmakers. Silks, satins, velvets and other fancy fabrics are found in many quilts, and a number of special cotton weaves were also widely used, such as cretonne (1880s-1920s), cotton flannel (circa 1875-circa 1925), cotton sateen (1930s-1940s), and feedsacking (1890s-1940s).

Shirtings, good-quality cottons that were generally white or cream with a plaid, check or print design, were popular from about 1875 to the 1920s. Lower-quality shirting indicates a later, 20th-century date. Many utilitarian quilts were made from wool, particularly between the 1860s and 1900.

PATTERNS

Quilt patterns offer a limited criterion for dating. Most traditional quilt patterns have been made for decades, if not centuries, but there are a few that can help pinpoint a date. Quilts made using the English paper piecing method (see "Techniques," below), such as Tumbling Blocks and Hexagons, are still being made. However, they were particularly popular in the United States during the last quarter of the 1800s, when they were made mainly from fancy fabrics, and again in the 1930s, when Grandmother's Flower Garden, created from hexagons, were widely made, though usually in cotton.

Four-block quilts, in which four, large, identical appliquéd blocks are joined edge-to-edge and bordered, enjoyed their heyday between 1870 and 1900. Crazy Quilts, especially those made from fancy scraps, were most popular during the last quarter of the 1800s. Redwork and other similar embroidered quilts were fashionable from about 1876 until after World War I.

Sunbonnet Sue and her myriad variations, both male and female, originated as an embroidery pattern in the 1880s, but the zenith of the design's popularity came in the 1920s and '30s. Double Wedding Ring, Dresden Plate and a variety of Fan patterns were widely made between the two world wars, as were kit quilts, which were mainly appliquéd. Yo-yo coverlets were in vogue during the same period, the 1920s and '30s, while Cathedral Window, another folded technique also called Mayflower, was more popular after 1950. All of these patterns are still in the lexicon of traditional quiltmakers, but looking closely at fabrics, colors and other aspects will help place a date on most examples.

TECHNIQUE

As with patterns, trying to date a quilt according to its technique is a vexed affair. Of course, all quilts finished before the patenting of the first commercially viable sewing machine, in 1846, were made by hand. But hand sewing, both for assembly and quilting, continues today. However, many vintage quilts were made by machine; it became an indication of a household's wealth if quilts were assembled and/or quilted by machine. Straight machine stitch was sometimes used for appliqué work. Such examples are probably vintage, as most modern machine appliqué would be applied with a zigzag stitch.

One-patch quilts are often made using the English paper piecing method, in which the shape is cut to the finished size from paper and a slightly larger fabric shape is basted to it to facilitate assembly. Vintage versions of this pattern were popular during the last quarter of the 1800s, particularly those made from silk, velvet and other dressmaking scraps.

Occasionally a top will appear with the papers still inside, and they can give an indication of age. Be wary, however, since paper was, like fabric, a valuable commodity and could have been set aside for years before being cut into backing papers for a quilt.

Square or rectangular fabric foundations of muslin or old shirting were often used to mount patterns such as Log Cabin and string-pieced quilts, as well as Crazy quilts, from about 1875 until the beginning of the 20th century. Strips or scraps were applied by hand or machine to the foundations, which were occasionally cut from old newspapers instead of fabric, and the squares were then assembled. If a quilt has worn spots, you can see the foundation material through the hole. This method is sometimes called press piecing, because each strip was pressed to the front after it was applied.

Hand appliqué is generally worked with an invisible stitch (see "Workmanship," below), but decorative embroidery stitches are sometimes found, especially on quilts from the 1930s and '40s such as Sunbonnet Sue.

THE FOUR B'S: BORDERS, BINDING, BATTING AND BACKING

These elements of a quilt can all give limited clues to its age and origin. Be careful in your assessment, though, because many quilts that were begun by one maker ended up being finished by another, often years later. A top completed in this way may have newer fabric used for borders and binding, as well as a new back, than the materials used for the rest of the quilt, although some tops are found together with the maker's planned backing.

Borders frame a quilt. Those made from simple strips are most often found, and give little help with dating. Appliquéd borders were popular after 1840, while scalloped borders are found most often on quilts from the 1920s until about 1950.

Binding encloses the edges of the quilt. There are two early binding methods. One was to turn the closely trimmed edges of both the top and the back to the inside, with one covering the batting. The edges were then seamed shut, and often a fringe was enclosed, especially before the Civil War. Crazy quilts from the Victorian era are also finished with this method, called knife-edge, and have fringe or lace decorating the edges. The other early method, called self-binding, involves turning the backing fabric to the front and stitching it in place to cover the batting and the edge of the quilt top. Both methods are still used today.

Separate bindings are also widely found on vintage quilts. A quilt bound with twill tape was probably made before 1860, while bias binding indicates a 20th-century example. Straight bindings are found on quilts from all periods. Some quilts have a decorative edging, such as prairie points—small folded triangles of cloth—popular after 1925.

Bindings are the first element to wear out on most quilts, and the first to be replaced. A seller who has replaced any part of a quilt should always tell a prospective customer.

Batting is the filling layer between the top and the back of a quilt. Quilts made before the invention of synthetic batting in the 1950s are batted with cotton or wool, but old blankets or quilts are sometimes found in place of batting fibers.

Before a company called Stearns & Foster made the first commercial cotton batting in 1846, the wool or cotton fibers were placed on the backing fabric and spread out as evenly as possible by hand. The top was added and basted in place, and the entire piece was then quilted. To keep the fibers from shifting during use or laundering, the quilting was worked in small stitch and very closely spaced rows. Polyester batting is widely used in quilts dating after 1960, and blends of polyester and cotton date from the 1990s.

Backing fabrics give few clues to the age of most quilts, though there are some exceptions. A quilt with a plaid cotton flannel back was probably made between 1875 and 1920. Silk show quilts from the last quarter of the 19th century often have backs made from lengths of dressmaking silks seamed to make up the width.

Large pieces of feedsacking sewn together to make a full back place a quilt between about 1890 and 1940, though printed feedsacks are generally found on quilts from the 1930s and '40s. Occasionally a printed back can help date the piece when taken in conjunction with the fabrics in the quilt top, but the fact remains that most quilt backs are made from muslin or plain cotton.

QUILTING

Quilting is another clue to age, though it is also limited in the information it can impart. Vintage whitework quilts, made using a method called *trapunto* or stuffed work, were generally made before the Civil War. Quilts made before commercial batting was available are quilted in close-worked rows and intricate designs. Outline quilting is found only on quilts from the 20th century.

Tied quilts are almost all utilitarian, the exception being thick quilts made from heavy wool or sometimes velvet, or quilts batted with a blanket. Machine quilting can occasionally be found on quilts from the second half of the 19th century, but is mainly a technique used in the 20th century, and particularly in the second half of the 1900s.

COLORS AND DYES

Because of the vagaries of dyeing fabric, color as imparted by a dye can offer clues to the age of a quilt. Spending time learning about the types of dyes will be well rewarded. Color has been added to cloth using natural dyestuffs since pre-history. The sources were vegetable, animal or mineral until chemical aniline dyes were discovered in 1856.

Many natural blues and blacks were derived from two related plants, indigo and logwood. *Woad*—the common name of the flowing plant *Isatis tinctoria*—was another source for blue hues lighter than the deep richness of indigo. The madder plant, native to Asia Minor, was the main source of certain reds and browns, while cochineal, a Central American insect, gave another source of red.

Butternut and white walnut, as well as the bark from many other trees, provided alternative ways to produce browns. In the 1820s a brown dye from manganese was introduced. Its hues were richer in value than the plant-based browns, but many of these dyes ate away the cloth, leaving holes wherever the brown should be.

Yellows came mainly from a West Indian tree called fustic, and purples were derived from a Mediterranean lichen called *orchil*. Dock was used to make a light green, which was mainly yellow. Most pre-aniline vegetable and mineral greens came from over-dying yellow with indigo or another blue. Many other substances have been used to dye fabric, from onionskins to pokeberry and lead chromate.

The main problems with most natural dyes are their lack of colorfastness and the fugitive nature of many of them. To overcome the lack of colorfastness, metallic compounds called *mordants* are added to the dye to make the color stick to the fibers of the cloth. When aniline dyes were discovered, dyes became more stable, and new colors were introduced, including a range of greens that had not been possible to achieve with natural plants.

Unfortunately, many of the chemical greens also faded. While we can regret the loss of the original color and intention of the maker, such fabrics can give clues to date, which is mainly the last quarter of the 1800s. Studying the section on Color in Liz Aleshire and Kathleen Barach's *Official Price Guide to Quilts* (2003, second edition) will repay dividends.

Getting an appraisal

There are many reasons to have quilts, both antique or collectible examples and new ones, appraised. An appraiser's report is necessary in a number of situations. Valuables should be insured, and a homeowner's insurance policy may need to be increased to cover a quilt collection.

If you decide to sell part or all of a collection, you need to know the fair market value of each item. If you are donating to a public collection such as a museum or historical society, your subsequent tax deduction depends on the appraised value of the gifts. If you lend your quilts for exhibition, and heaven forbid something happens to them, the United States Post Office requires an appraiser's report to repay its full value.

As you become more familiar with what constitutes value regarding quilts in your collection, your increasing knowledge of fabrics, colors, condition, workmanship and all the other determining factors will help you to decide if a quilt purchase is a good deal. An appraiser's eye will help you confirm your instincts, and some sellers will allow you to commission an appraisal before you purchase.

Finding an appraiser is similar to finding any service provider. Friends, colleagues and other collectors can often recommend a qualified appraiser. The Internet has become a vast network of information, and simply Googling "quilt appraiser" will lead you to menus that allow you to look for a professional close to your home base. Local museums or historical societies that have quilts in their collections and local quilt guilds will almost certainly know of appraisers in your area.

The Internet is also useful in helping you understand exactly what an appraiser should do. Training to become an appraiser is an arduous process requiring many hours of study, and the societies that are responsible for examining and certifying their members have strict standards for qualification and codes of ethics. Make sure that an appraiser you are considering is certified and up to date with the new information that is constantly being disseminated. She or he should abide by the ethical code of conduct as required by his or her society.

There might be a discrepancy between the fee for an appraisal for insurance purposes and one for determining fair market value, but it is probably best to get both as long as you are going through the process. Among the things you should ask for are a fee based on a flat rate for appraising a specific number of quilts, or a charge per quilt.

Some appraisers may ask for an hourly fee, especially if they feel that the quilt will need to be researched heavily for some reason, but bear in mind that this cost could be higher than agreeing to a flat fee. You will need a written report for each quilt appraised. A verbal report, which should be less expensive than a full written one, might be adequate if you are just curious about a quilt or two, but it will not satisfy an insurance or tax claim.

There are standard forms for recording the information, which should include not just facts about the quilt, but also details of the appraiser's qualification and experience.

Bear in mind that quilts, like any other collectible, are subject to the whims of fashion, which can affect availability. A style that was all the rage among interior decorators who snapped up many of the best examples as they came on the market can become passé overnight. A type of quilt that had languished, ignored for decades, can take its place with equal speed. Condition can change, regrettably usually for the worse. Hence, values can change over time, and a reassessment of a collection should be carried out from time to time.

Insuring your quilts

While quilts are not the prime target of most household burglars, they sometimes do get stolen or suffer from disasters ranging from fire or flood to damage when on display in an exhibition. Any collection should be insured.

Some insurance companies include a certain level of coverage as part of a basic homeowner's policy, but if your collection is particularly extensive or valuable, it probably won't be covered in full. Your agent can tell you what coverage you have and help you decide if you need to increase it, and a qualified appraiser can assess and evaluate your collection to make sure you have adequate insurance.

Keeping a Collection

Repair or finish?

Among the enduring questions for collectors is whether to repair damage on vintage quilts and finish tops. The debate will no doubt continue to rage, and it is up to the individual collector to decide how to treat a collection. Some people buy damaged quilts with the intention of repairing them to stabilize and preserve them, even in an altered form, for the future.

Others find a professional who will carry out repairs for a fee. Some simply put such purchases in storage to decide about later. The important thing about any of these options is to arrest the pace of deterioration while remaining true to the maker's original intention. For this reason, most repairs should be made as nearly as possible with fabric of the same vintage as the original, and the old fabric, where it exists, should be left in place, with the repair applied on top.

Cutter quilts (*see page 10-11*) can provide a source of vintage fabrics if you hit on a lucky find. If you can't or don't wish to replace worn or torn areas, it is possible to apply a layer of virtually transparent fine-weave tulle over the damage to keep it from suffering more from handling. This stabilization should always be carried out on quilts that will be dry-cleaned (see below).

Many beautiful and pristine quilt tops are available or in private hands, including a number in this book, and several of the quilts featured are tops that have been completed in the hands of the collector. Some collectors especially like tops because they take up less storage space than finished quilts, and many of us find being able to see the construction, especially on pieced examples, enlightening and fascinating.

If you decide to finish a top, look for damage and repair those areas before you do anything else. If the top has no border, decide whether to add one or more, and look for fabrics that fit the time period. The same goes for the binding, as well as the backing, though muslin will almost always work. Binding fabric and method should be chosen carefully, too, so you'll need to know something about the time period when the top was made.

Quilting patterns should also be in keeping with the quilt's era. If your top has the quilting already marked, that decision is already made, and you can be sure it follows the maker's intention! Finished vintage tops are generally more expensive than unfinished ones, but they are less costly than a quilt finished at the same time as the top. Just make sure the additions are documented and the dates are recorded accurately. The date technically should be stated as the date when the quilt was actually finished, but it is important to record the date of the top as well.

Some collectors remove portions of a quilt that they feel are out of keeping with other examples of the same type or time frame, or simply are unattractive as the result of poor workmanship or unfortunate color choices. Although these reworked quilts cannot be claimed as authentically vintage, and almost certainly don't adhere to the original maker's ideas, they are often more attractive than the original.

Badly executed quilting, a poor choice of thread or color, sashing or borders that are so out of true that they override the attractive aspects of the piece are all given as reasons to remake such quilts or tops. These changes should be correctly documented and the quilt dated accordingly in the collector's records.

Sets of quilt blocks or cutout pieces of vintage fabrics often come on the market, especially on Internet sales. It seems our ancestors also had UFOs (UnFinished Objects, for the non-quilting collector) just like today's quilters. These pieces of the past can provide fascinating glimpses into the history of textiles and into the techniques used by our forebears. They can also be assembled if you wish.

As with any repairs or finishing, you should aim to use appropriate fabrics and match the techniques of the originals. If you need to make a few more blocks to go with vintage hand-sewn ones, they should be hand stitched, although sashing and borders could be added by machine. Cutout pieces such as the ones used to make the Fan quilt on *page 11* can be put together to become vintage quilts for future collectors to treasure.

Cleaning

Cleaning a vintage quilt, whether it is a new acquisition that needs washing or an existing part of a collection that has been subjected to the stresses and strains of daily life, should be approached carefully. Every quilt should be assessed individually before any cleaning is attempted. Some stains are best left in the quilt, but others may cause additional damage if they are not removed.

The age of a quilt is less of a factor than its overall condition and the type of fabrics and batting used. Most experts do not recommend dry cleaning cotton or linen quilts, although I was successful with this method on a 19th-century cotton whitework quilt that had suffered some surface staining during a house move. Silk and wool quilts may leave you with no option other than dry cleaning, but do some research and try to find an establishment with experience handling vintage textiles. A dealer or fellow collector might be able to recommend a suitable place.

Museum conservation departments are usually helpful if you contact them, or check with a national trade organization. If a cotton quilt is not colorfast and has no breaks in the fabrics, one way to clean it yourself is to hold the upholstery nozzle of your vacuum cleaner a few inches above the fabric with the machine set on low. If you cover each area of the quilt with a clean piece of fine-mesh screening as you work, you will minimize potential damage to loose thread or bearded batting.

If washing a quilt seems to be the only option for cleaning it, approach the task very carefully. There is almost no circumstance in which most experts would consider machine-washing a vintage quilt to be a good idea. Before laundering by hand, make sure all the fabrics are colorfast.

To be absolutely thorough, first rub a dry piece of white cotton over the fabric being tested. If the color transfers to the white cloth, the fabric is not colorfast. If no color is picked up, dampen the cloth with cool water and rub again. If this test is passed, drip a few drops of barely warm water on each fabric to be tested. Blot the area, and if the color transfers to it, abandon the idea of washing the quilt. If the cotton stays white, the color probably won't run, but this is never a certainty.

If you decide to risk washing, consider the batting as well. Old cotton batting will lump together in some circumstances, and wool batting will shrink, often dramatically, if it gets wet. Quilts with wool batting should only be dry-cleaned.

If you decide to wash a quilt, most experts recommend washing it in the bathtub, unless you have access to a tub large enough to lay the quilt flat. Few of us do, so you'll need to fold the quilt as many times as necessary to fit it in a tub of barely warm water. Nancy O'Bryant Puentes places a sheet in the water to line the tub and places the quilt in the tub, carefully fan-pleating it.

Allow it to soak for up to 12 hours, changing the water as each tubful looks dirty. If necessary, add a gentle, natural washing solution to the water. Rinsing properly is a time-consuming process, and you will have to drain and refill the tub several times to remove all the cleaning solution.

After she has rinsed thoroughly, Ms. Puentes leaves quilts in the tub for several hours to drain as much water as possible before she lifts them out, using the sheet to take much of the weight. Get help to lift and carry it if necessary. Water is heavy, and the weight can cause lasting damage to you and the quilt if it is mishandled, and for this reason vintage quilts should not be dried on a clothesline or in a tumble dryer. Flat is best here, too, and outdoors is the best place to accomplish this part of the process.

Most people spread clean sheets in the shade on the grass or a deck or patio and lay the quilt flat on them. Blotting the quilt with towels will take up even more water. Then cover the quilt with another clean sheet to protect it from outdoor mishaps. You can turn it over once the upright side feels dry. Replace the sheets with dry ones and let it dry completely.

Storing your quilts

One question that is always asked when I talk to an audience about my collection is, "Where do you keep all your quilts?" The best way to store quilts is flat. Some museums have shallow drawers in which they keep their most fragile and valuable quilts, but the space needed to flat-store an entire collection is usually not available even to large institutions. Since storing completely flat is not possible in my house, or in most others, I use the next-best place, which is on a spare bed, for my fragile and valuable treasures.

The bed of course gets used from time to time, so this method is not ideal, either, since no one can sleep under 40 or 50 quilts. I also combine folding and rolling some of my less precious quilts and keep them in glass-fronted Victorian-era lawyer's bookcases, tops on the inside to keep them from getting dusty. Acid-free tissue paper keeps them from touching the wood, and protects the folds, and the quilts add to the room's decor.

Options for safe storage include acid-free storage boxes, which can be ordered from suppliers of archival storage. The same suppliers also sell acid-free paper. The boxes are relatively expensive, but each usually holds two or three quilts. The problem they present for many people is finding a place to store the boxes themselves.

Ideally, we would all have room to have special quilt storage rooms with floor-to-ceiling shelving sized specifically for our archival boxes. Basements and attics are not recommended for obvious reasons—extreme temperature fluctuations, and potential dampness or flooding.

Storing quilts in plastic bags should never be an option, either, because plastic traps moisture inherent in any fabric and can lead to mildew and rotting. Folded quilts can be stored neatly by wrapping them in cotton muslin or slipping them into cotton pillowcases, but remember to put tissue paper along the folds.

Some collectors and institutions roll their quilts on heavy-duty cardboard tubing, which can save space but is thought by many textile experts to put undue strain on the fabrics and the batting. If you use this method, wrap the tube with acid-free paper and roll the quilt with the top out to keep surface wrinkles to a minimum. Cover the quilt with a layer of acid-free tissue so that as you roll, no fabric is touching another. You can put more than one quilt on a tube, layering tissue between each quilt.

Rolls should be stored horizontally, which creates another challenge to finding adequate space. Some collectors attach the rolls to a wall using display methods employed by carpet stores and upholstery fabric suppliers.

Keep your storage areas clear of pests as you would anywhere in your home. Moths, mice and crawling insects like silverfish can wreak havoc on fabrics, and they love dark, undisturbed places.

If you display your quilts, you should rotate them occasionally, which means that you will be folding and unfolding from time to time. This is good for your collection, but try to make sure that you fold each quilt in a different configuration if possible to keep from creating permanent fold lines. If you don't take your quilts out of storage on a regular basis, try setting aside an annual date to take them out and give them an airing. This will give you a chance to check for damage and refold them.

Displaying your quilts

For me the best way to display a quilt is to use it on a bed. Choose quilts that will withstand the rigors of daily living, and if you sleep under a quilt, vintage or not, use a sheet between it and the bodies in the bed. While you probably don't want more than one or two quilts on your bed, those that are slept in irregularly can be layered creatively with two or more quilts of the same color palette or pattern.

Many quilts can be used decoratively as throws over the backs of chairs or couches to great effect. Make sure they are out of direct sunlight, though, and refold them after giving them a good shake occasionally to get rid of dust. Banisters also make good places to display quilts, but the rules about refolding and about light and dust still apply.

Some quilts can be effective on occasional tables or piano tops, a la the Victorians, but cover tables used to hold drinks or cups of coffee with protective glass cut to size.

Wooden quilt or towel racks can be attractive features in almost any room in the house, and are especially good for displaying small quilts and tops. Wall-hung quilts should be placed where they receive little light, either natural or artificial, are away from cooking and other food preparation areas, and out of rooms with open fireplaces where smoke damage can occur. They should be hung on systems that carry the weight evenly and are made in a way that protects fabrics from direct contact with wood.

A hanging sleeve about 4 inches wide can be added to any quilt that will be hung. Another option is a system favored by many museums—using Velcro™ applied to the top edge of the quilt and married to its Velcro counterpart anchored to the wall. Quilts that hang should be rotated regularly. Most textile experts recommend no more than six months of hanging without a rest and allowing a hiatus of an equal or greater amount of time.

Experts disagree about the wisdom of framing a quilt. While glass or Plexiglas™ frames do keep dust out, they can lead to trapped moisture. Framed quilts should have spacer blocks inserted inside the frames to keep the transparent material from touching the fabric, and the backs should not be sealed. Stella Rubin recommends using a layer of cotton instead of cardboard as the back.

Enjoying Your Collection

Remember that collecting should be fun. We should of course stay within our budgets. We should all follow the advice of most experienced collectors and buy only what we love. Sometimes we get carried away, but a number of dealers started as collectors who decided at some point to sell part of their holdings.

Selling part of a collection is known in the museum world as de-accessioning, and while it shouldn't be undertaken lightly, it is an acceptable way to make room for new treasures.

Above all, we can be learning while we preserve the past, and enjoying the journeys, both the physical search as we look for new acquisitions and the emotional trip as we educate ourselves and others.

Warman's Vintage Quilts Identification & Price Guide contains only quilts in private hands. At the time of writing, none of the quilts pictured are in public collections or museums. The book would not have been possible without the willing and generous participation of the following private collectors and dealers:

Sylvia & Paul Adair

Gail Bakkom

Linda Reuss Benson

Diane & Bruce Boucher

Donna Bowen

Carol Butzke

Patricia Cox

Luella & Jed Doss

Henry Drewal,
  the Siddi Women's Quilting Cooperative

Nina & Richard Edelman

Nancy Gorens Edelman

Carol Johnson Fritz

Annette Hooker

Deanna Jaloviar

Michael Kerr, Michael Kerr Gallery

Terri Sankovitz Kirchner &
  Margaret Mathews Sankovitz

Chris Lynn Kirsch

Judy Zoelzer Levine

Tink & Dick Linhart

The late Vicki Maloney

Jane Barclay Mandel

Jeanne Peterson

Lisbeth & Gary Rattner

Maribeth Schmit

I thank them all most profoundly.

For further information regarding any of the quilts, please contact me through my website www.maggigordon.com.

The Michael Kerr Gallery specializes in antique ethnographic material, including African American quilts and Japanese textiles. Michael Kerr can be contacted at kerrethno@mac.com.

The Siddi Women's Quilting Cooperative can be contacted through Henry Drewal at hjdrewal@wisc.edu.

CHAPTER 2
PATCHWORK QUILTS

While patchwork is probably as old as sewing itself, the patchwork, or pieced, quilt used as a bedcover is only a few hundred years old, and the majority of existing examples date from the latter half of the 19th century on. By the 17th century the traditional techniques of quiltmaking as we know them were widely practiced in Europe, and were carried to the New World by the colonists who ventured to North America. Many changes of style took place as this new world clashed and then reconciled with the old, and quilting fads and fashions came and went, leaving a legacy that gives collectors a treasure trove from which to choose.

The following section is divided by style or type of quilt. Several categories in the section are sub-divided to cover as broad a range of possibilities as space allows.

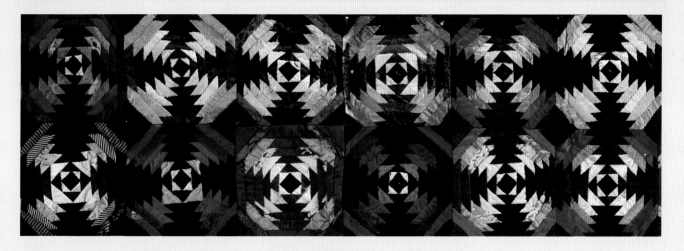

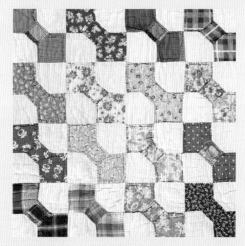

In this chapter

24 Wholecloth, Strippies and Frames
34 Strips and Strings
40 Log Cabin
55 One-Patch
71 Traditional Blocks
112 Representational Blocks
141 Signatures
147 Curves

Wholecloth, Strippies and Frames

Wholecloth quilts are among the earliest type used as bedcovers. The name suggests that they are made from one single piece of cloth, but the narrow width of 18th- and 19th-century textiles means that most are technically pieced—strips are joined selvage to selvage to make the piece wide enough to cover a bed. They are then backed with a similar piece of fabric, batted and quilted through all three layers.

The quality of the quilting, including the design, is the main determining factor in a quilt's appeal and value. Found only in wealthy households, wholecloth quilts were made from cotton (often chintz), wool and silk, and could be printed or solid color. The most refined were known as Whitework, made from a plain white fabric, usually cotton. The design of the quilting was most often medallion-style, with a motif in the center surrounded by wreaths or cables or floral garlands.

Clamshell, crosshatch, and parallel lines are used to fill in blank areas. The quilting is closely worked; this was the way in which the loose batting fibers were held in place to prevent bunching and lumping inside the fabric layers. Though it is possible to find them in various parts of the country, the best place to look for Wholecloth quilts is in New England and the mid-Atlantic regions. Such quilts were made primarily in those areas, which had become stable and well established by the early 1800s.

Strippy quilts had their origins in England, primarily in the northeastern counties of Durham and Northumberland, but their graphic qualities and ease of assembly made them popular elsewhere. Home sewing machines were fairly common by the late 19th century and fabric was priced within the reach of most quiltmakers, so combining strips of contrasting fabrics was a simple way to make a quilt quickly.

It was also an economical way to work a more expensive fabric like chintz into a quilt. Some pieces were quilted in an all-over pattern, much like the designs found on Wholecloth quilts, but most were stitched in strips with a variety of patterns. British versions tend to feature non-pieced strips in two or more different fabrics, while American versions are more likely to be made from strips of pieced blocks combined with alternating plain panels of a contrasting cloth.

The British style shows up in Amish Bars quilts, which are invariably of solid color, but unlike their English ancestors, Bars quilts almost always have a wide border. Among African American quilters, the style is known as Lazy Gal (see pages 234-235).

Frame quilts date from the same era as Wholecloth ones, and true frame quilts are a rarity seldom seen outside of museums. American quiltmakers never took to Frame quilts with the same enthusiasm as their British counterparts, but the style is found in U.S. quilts. The original British Frame quilts consisted of a central panel, or medallion, surrounded by a series of borders, or "frames." The center was usually a panel of some desirable cloth or an appliquéd motif, while the borders ranged from plain strips of contrasting fabrics to pieced blocks, which were usually based on squares, triangles and rectangles.

Intersecting corners were often pieced to add interest to the plain borders. American examples are of a later date, and reflect the style of an interesting center surrounded by borders, pieced or plain, but are visually different from the British style.

Amish Bars quilts often have pieced corners in the borders, too.

WHITEWORK QUILT

C 1825

Maker unknown. Philadelphia, Pennsylvania.
White cotton medallion-style with four-poster
cutouts in two corners; hand quilted rings and cables
in center surrounded by pairs of doves touching
beaks and with hand-embroidered eyelet eyes;
birds are framed with stitched "broderie anglaise"
embroidery, then a frame of crosshatch, then a wide
border of more broderie anglaise with swags and
floral motifs.

$3,000-$5,000

WHITEWORK QUILT

C 1875

Maker unknown. Britain.
White cotton seersucker-like weave top; hand-quilted
clamshell center, cabled borders; white muslin back;
knife-edge binding.

$1,000-$1,500

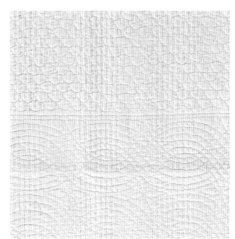

PAISLEY WHOLECLOTH

C 1880

Maker unknown. Northeastern England.
Red, black and fugitive-green paisley cotton; same top and back; knife-edge binding. Thick blanket batting. Hand quilted zigzag rows of red thread.

$600-$750

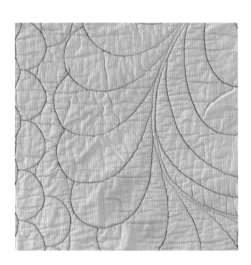

WILKERSON DIAMOND SCROLL QUILT

C 1925

Maker unknown. United States.
Pinkish-beige cotton sateen, hand quilted using a pattern from the Wilkerson Art Co. Crosshatch center, scroll frame surrounded by clamshell; scalloped edges. Cotton back; bias binding. Over-dyed by the present owner to remove a stain, resulting in a color often used by Wilkerson for this pattern.

$750-$1,000

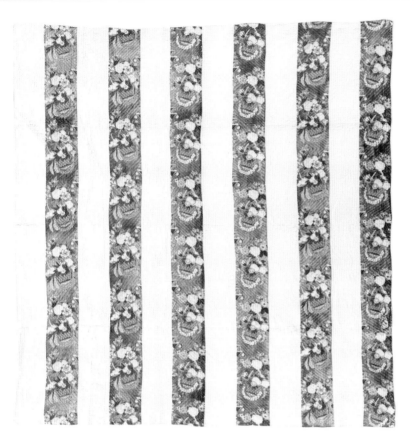

CHINTZ STRIPPY

Dated 1841 in ink

Maker Mary Raymond? Signature is faded and only partially legible. Mt.??, Ohio.

Faded chintz strips alternating with muslin strips. Cotton batting. Muslin back; muslin binding. Closely worked, hand-quilted diagonal lines on chintz, leafy vine on muslin. Some staining on back.

$1,500-$2,000

STRIPPY QUILT

C 1880

Maker unknown. Northeast England.

Red and white cotton solids. Muslin back; knife-edge binding. Hand-quilted crosshatch in red strips, running cables in white strips.

$1,500-$2,000

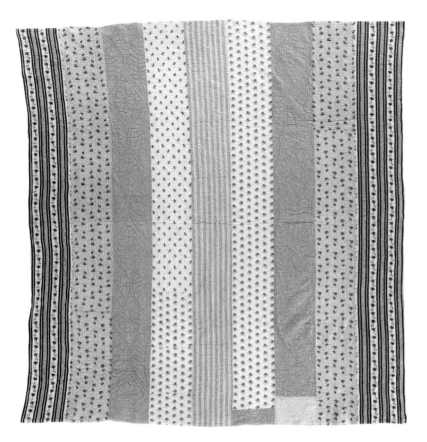

PRINT STRIPPY QUILT

C 1880

Maker unknown. Durham, Northeast England.
Cotton print strips, several pieced to make up the
length. Muslin back; knife-edge binding. Hand
quilted Weardale chain and daisies.

$600-$750

PRINT STRIPPY

C 1900

Maker unknown. Northeast England.
Pink and blue cotton print strips. Batting is an older
quilt. Double-quilted muslin back; knife-edge
binding. Hand quilted through top and older quilt
with crosshatch.

$600-$750

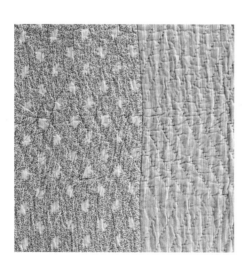

CHINESE COINS STRIPPY TOP

C 1890

Maker unknown. United States.

Multicolored cotton prints, solids, mainly shirtings; one cheater patch; gray strips with dots and checks. Hand pieced.

$100-$250

SQUARE IN A SQUARE STRIPPY TOP

C 1880

Maker unknown. United States.

Possibly two makers: three strips are pieced squares in a square. Some damage.

Cotton prints and solids, mainly indigos for square blocks; cheddar strips and sashing; hand pieced.

$100 or less

TRIPLE X

C 1900
Maker unknown. Northeast England.
Pink and white cotton strips. Muslin back; knife-edge binding. Hand quilted cables in pink strips, cartwheels in white strips.

$750-$1,000

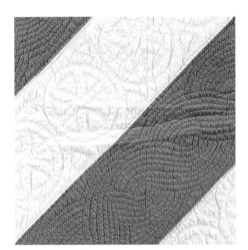

FRAME QUILT

C 1930
Maker unknown. United States.
Blue, yellow, pink and green cotton sateen solids; wide strips; mitered corners. Wool batting. Heavy muslin back; muslin binding. Hand quilted parallel lines and crosshatch.

$400-$600

ONE-PATCH SQUARES MEDALLION QUILT
20th century
Maker unknown. United States.
Gray, brown and tan wool squares set on point and framed with strips of wool. Wool batting.
Striped wool back. Back and binding worn. Machine quilted.
$400-$600

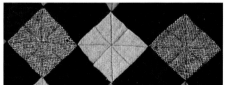

FOUR-PATCH FRAME QUILT

C 1930

Maker unknown. United States.

Multicolored cotton solids and prints assembled in four-patch blocks joined to make strips for frames; center rectangle with five-pieced frames and six white cotton frames. Muslin back; muslin binding. Hand quilted. Skillful piecing and quilting; well washed.

$400-$600

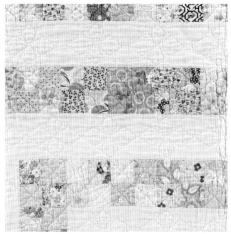

FRAME QUILT

C 1930

Maker unknown. United States.

Multicolored cotton prints and solids, mainly green and purple, white cotton; assembled in strips on point; pieced purple and white triangle border. Muslin back; muslin binding. Machine quilted in the ditch to make a diamond grid.

$250-$400

BOSTON COMMONS TOP

20th century

Maker unknown. United States.

Cotton prints and solids set on point in concentric rectangles; orange print border. Hand pieced.

$100-$250

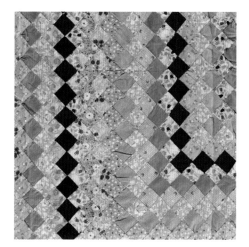

ANN ORR FLORAL WREATH MEDALLION

C 1935

Maker unknown. United States.

Multicolored cotton solids on white cotton backgrounds; blue and pink solid cotton sashing; blue cotton scalloped border. Muslin back; knife-edge binding. Hand quilted crosshatch with motifs in white sashing squares, clamshell on border.

$1,500-$2,000

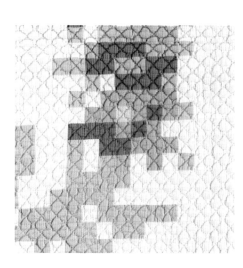

Strips and Strings

Strips of fabric can be joined in many ways to make interesting and pleasingly simple designs. In quiltmaking, strings are the long uneven scraps of fabric left over from dressmaking projects, and sewing them together to make a larger piece is an obvious way to using them efficiently and economically. The improvisational quality of the resulting fabric can give a quilt a liveliness that is hard to beat. String piecing is found in many African American quilts (see pages 235-247), but has been used in traditional European-style quilts to great effect for many years.

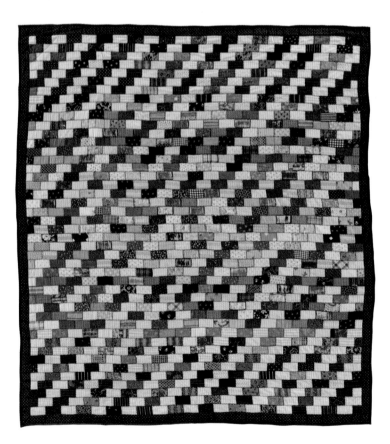

BRICK WALL

C 1890 (top)

Maker unknown. United States.

Rectangular cotton scraps: double pinks, clarets, indigos, Prussian blues, black and white mourning prints, ginghams, stripes, anchor print; brick wall setting arranged in light and dark diagonal rows; indigo border.

New red and white cotton print back; knife-edge binding; polyester batting. Hand-worked herringbone-stitch quilting, all 1970s.

$100-$250

RAIL FENCE

20th century

Maker unknown. United States.

Multicolored wool strips, seven per block, with striping alternating horizontally and vertically; two sides bordered with strips of "piano key" piecing. Gray-striped wool back; dark brown binding.

$250-$400

RAIL FENCE COVERLET

C 1910

Maker unknown. Midwestern United States.

Wool suiting scraps and cottons in alternating horizontal and vertical arrangement. No batting. Plaid cotton back; back-to-front self-binding embellished with herringbone stitch worked in red yarn. Minimal hand quilting in the ditch.

$250-$400

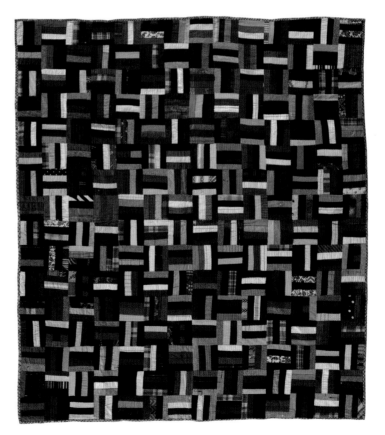

RAIL FENCE

C 1950

Maker Gertrude Miller for the owner. Brown Deer, Wisconsin.

Multicolored cotton scraps, mainly 1930s and '40s fabrics; wide purple border. Purple cotton back, purple binding.

$100-$250

STRING-PIECED FOUR-POINT STARS

C 1900

Maker unknown. United States.

Multicolored cotton scraps; hourglass centers with four string-pieced points; white cotton diamond spacers. Coarse white cotton back; back-to-front self-binding. Hand-quilted outline.

$250-$400

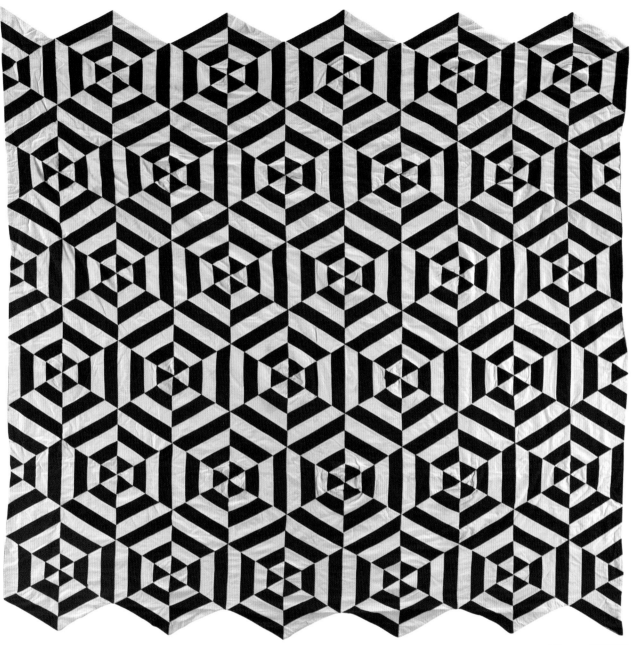

SPIDER'S WEB TOP

20th century

Maker unknown. United States.

Red and white cotton solids; strip pieced and backed for stability with a modern cotton print;

knife-edge binding.

$200–$400

SUGAR CONE THROW

C 1920

Maker unknown. United States.

Multicolored silk scraps with black and beige, worked on foundation blocks, which are visible. No batting. No backing; black binding.

$750-$1,000

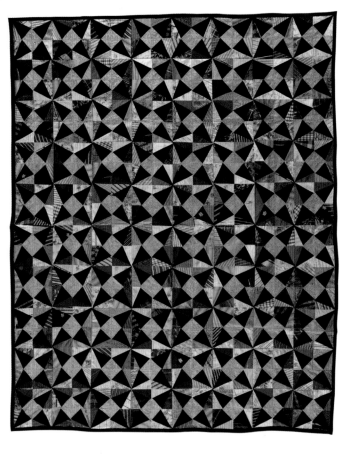

SUGAR CONE THROW

C 1920

Maker unknown (possibly the same as previous quilt). United States.

Multicolored silk scraps with pink and black; worked on foundation blocks, which are visible. No batting. No backing; knife-edge binding.

$750-$1,000

STRING-PIECED LE MOYNE STAR

Dated 1930 (embroidered in one corner)
Maker unknown. United States.
Multicolored dressmaking scraps of wool, velvet, cotton, sateen and silk string-pieced on muslin foundation; black velvet backgrounds; each scrap outlined in herringbone stitch; red sashing; black, red and tan pieced half-square triangle border. Lavender and blue paisley cotton flannel back; red cotton sateen binding. Hand-quilted crosshatch in star blocks, feather motif in sashing, parallel lines in border.
$750-$1,000

STRING-PIECED EIGHT-POINT STARS TOP

C 1940
Maker unknown. United States.
Multicolored cotton scraps string-pieced for stars, including many plaids and checks; backgrounds dark blue, red/blue checked or blue/white checked, alternating checkerboard style. Backed for stability.
$100 or less

Log Cabin

Log Cabin is the quintessential patchwork quilt block in the minds of most people. Its amazing versatility has been used to create quilts of astonishing variety and beauty for at least 200 years, but it is not, as many suppose, the personification of the American quilt. Nor was it named in honor of Abraham Lincoln, as romantic as the notion might seem.

The basic block is built as a series of "logs" around a center, traditionally red to represent the hearth at the heart of every home, but there are variations even to the basic construction. In Courthouse Steps, the strips are placed in sequence on opposite sides of the center; in Pineapple, the center becomes octagonal as strips are added on four sides of a square and then at an angle in each of the four corners.

There are even variations on the variations: the centers can be any geometric shape, or irregular, or pieced; the "center" can be moved into one corner and strips added on two sides; other shapes can be inserted at the ends of the strips to create "cornerstones" or "chimneys" or "flying geese."

And the versatility of Log Cabin doesn't stop with the block. Perhaps the way the blocks are organized, or "set," when the quilt is assembled is even more important than the style of the block. The main patterns are Light and Dark (or Sunshine and Shadow), Barn Raising, Straight Furrow and Pineapple, all of which are included in this section, but there are myriad variations to look out for.

Log Cabin quilts are made from cotton, silk, wool and blends, and from combinations of different kinds of fabric. The workmanship ranges from exquisite to strictly utilitarian, and the best examples feature strong contrasts in value between the light and dark areas. Because so many Log Cabin quilts were made, they are relatively common, both as finished quilts and as tops. Tops allow collectors to see the various construction methods that were used, from simple strips sewn together by hand to logs machine-stitched onto a foundation of muslin or shirting squares.

SILK SUNSHINE AND SHADOW LOG CABIN

C 1880

Maker unknown. Yorkshire, England.
Multicolored silk ribbon logs; black velvet centers with embroidered flowers. Back is brown machine quilted cotton with a thick batting, possibly a blanket or an older quilt. Edges on top and bottom are turned inside to enclose a handmade 7"-wide lace edging. Some shattering.

$750-$1,000

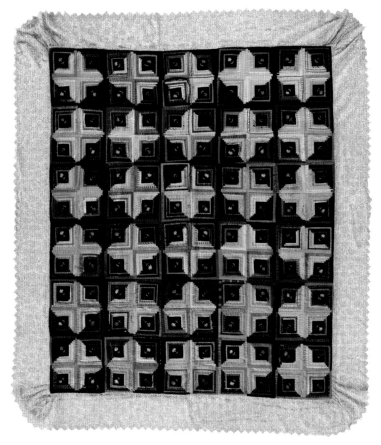

SUNSHINE AND SHADOW LOG CABIN

20th century

Maker unknown. United States, probably Midwest. Unusual setting, well planned and executed. Mainly wool solids for logs; green or red velvet centers. Wool batting. Gray wool back; bias plaid binding, machine applied.

$750-$1,000

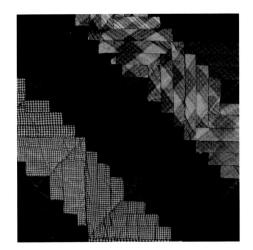

SUNSHINE AND SHADOW LOG CABIN TOP

C 1900

Maker unknown. Wisconsin.

Cotton shirtings, indigos, plaids, stripes, prints for logs; red cotton centers; machine pieced, no foundations. Some damage.

$100-$250

SUNSHINE AND SHADOW LOG CABIN

C 1900

Maker unknown. United States.

Cotton solids and prints, mainly cadet blues, indigos, red and white prints, and brown-and-white prints. Blue and pink floral cotton print back; blue binding. Hand quilted: diagonal and horizontal lines.

$100-$250

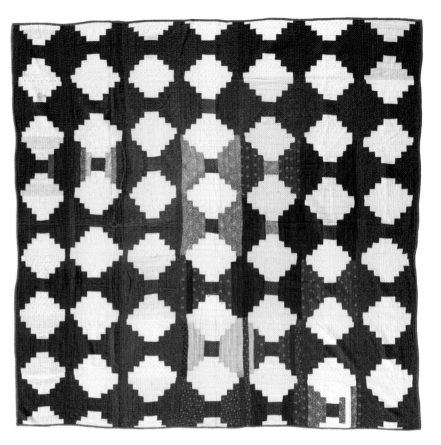

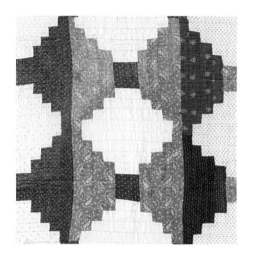

BARN RAISING LOG CABIN

C 1900

Maker unknown. United States.

Wool solids and prints for logs; solid red wool centers. Brown print wool challis back; two sides back-to-front self-binding, two sides red wool binding.

$400-$600

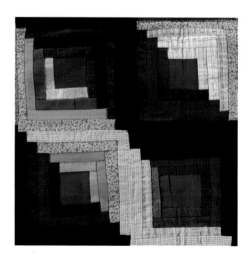

BARN RAISING LOG CABIN

C 1900

Maker unknown. United States.

Multicolored wool and silk logs, in light rows strips of red alternating with light fabrics; centers pieced light and dark. Brown-and-gray wool plaid back; black binding. Tied to the back. Some shattered silks.

$400–$600

BARN RAISING LOG CABIN

C 1900

Maker unknown. United States.

Multicolored cotton logs; tan centers. Wool batting.
Red-and-black cotton print back: back-to-front self-
binding, very frayed.

$400-$600

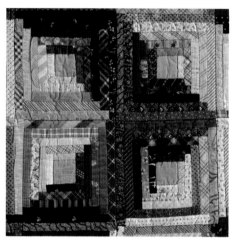

OFFSET BARN RAISING LOG CABIN TOP

C 1900

Maker unknown. United States.

Multicolored cotton prints and solids, many shirtings,
machine stitched on shirting foundations; solid red
cotton centers.

$250-$400

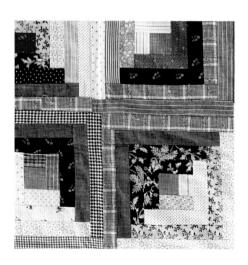

SQUARE SET BARN RAISING LOG CABIN

C 1860

Maker unknown. United States, probably Midwest.
Wool solids for logs; black wool centers; blocks set on
point. Plaid wool back; black binding.

$750–$1,000

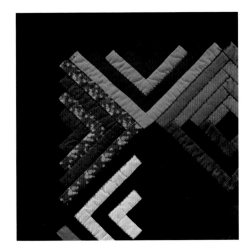

SQUARE SET BARN RAISING LOG CABIN

C 1875

Maker unknown. Canada.
Wool solids and prints for logs; red centers. Black
binding.

$750–$1,000

COURTHOUSE STEPS LOG CABIN

1930s

Maker unknown. Virginia.

Red, yellow, pink and green cotton solids for logs; pieced centers of two triangle squares; hand pieced; turquoise border. Green cotton back; back-to-front self-binding. Hand-quilted diamond grid.

$750-$1,000

COURTHOUSE STEPS

C 1900

Maker unknown. United States.

Multicolored cottons, darks mainly indigos; red centers. Striped cotton beard guard sewn to top end. Gray cotton back (very frayed); red binding, probably new, zigzag-stitched in place.

$250-$400

COURTHOUSE STEPS TOP

C 1880

Maker unknown. United States.

Red and white cotton solids; red cotton border; blocks are hand pieced, top is assembled by machine. Some color loss and loose seams.

$100-$250

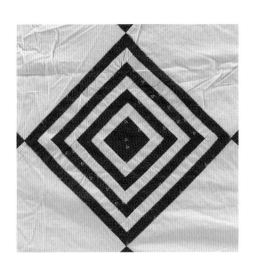

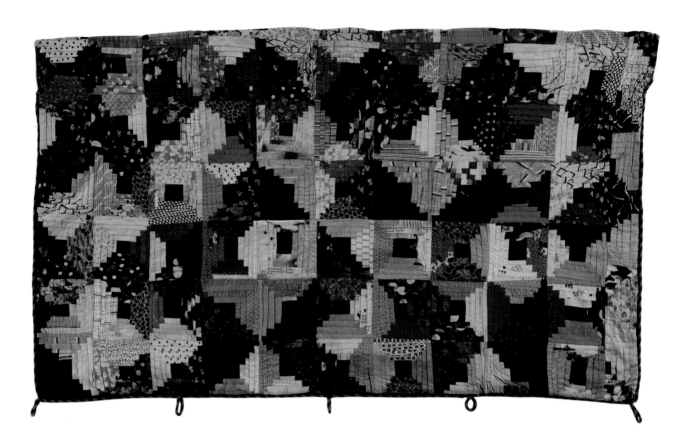

COURTHOUSE STEPS THROW

C 1900

Maker unknown. United States.

Multicolored silk logs, mainly black centers.

Embroidered blanket back; knife-edge binding
finished with heavy upholstery cord, tassels added to
bottom edge.

$400-$600

STRAIGHT FURROW LOG CABIN

C 1870

Maker unknown. United States.

Cotton prints and solids; red cotton centers. Gray and tan cotton stripe back; back-to-front self-binding. No quilting.

$600-$750

STRAIGHT FURROW LOG CABIN

19th century

Maker unknown. United States.

Multicolored silks and velvets; red or brown velvet centers. Silk print back; brown velvet binding.

$600-$750

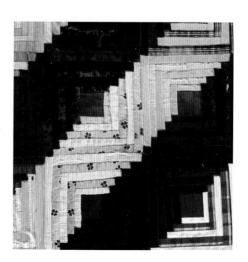

VERTICAL STRAIGHT FURROW LOG CABIN

C 1925

Maker unknown. Northeastern United States. Peach, rose, and khaki silk solids for logs; tan silk centers. Green wool back; back-to-front self-binding. Tied with floss in centers of blocks.

$600-$750

STRAIGHT FURROW LOG CABIN TOP

C 1890

Maker unknown. United States.

Multicolored wool gabardine prints and solids: Lancaster blues, red and black, madders, paisleys, butterscotch, double pinks for logs; red centers; hand pieced to muslin foundations.

$400-$600

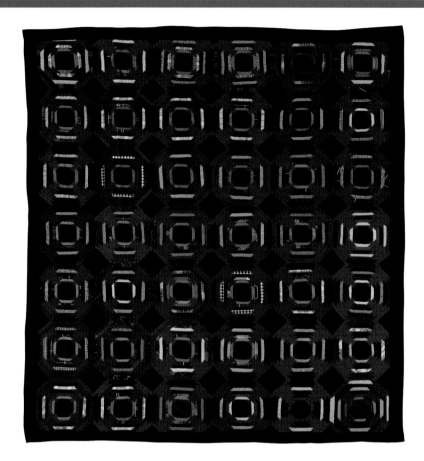

PINEAPPLE LOG CABIN

C 1880

Maker unknown. United States.

Mixed fabrics in prints and solids, predominantly reds and blacks; hand pieced; black wool border. No batting. Red and black cotton print back; front-to-back black binding. No quilting.

$750-$1,000

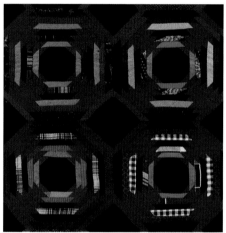

PINEAPPLE LOG CABIN

C 1880

Maker unknown. United States.

Wool and cotton prints, predominantly lights with red-and-blue centers; hand pieced; pieced border of narrow diagonal stripes. Cotton print back. No quilting.

$750-$1,000

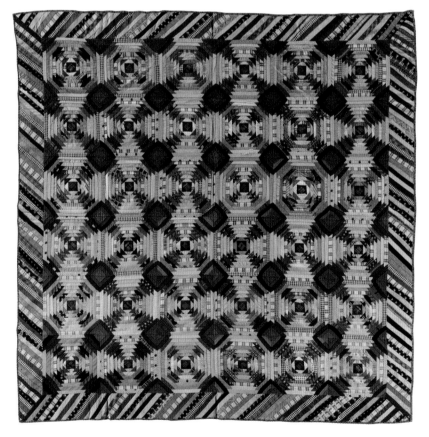

PINEAPPLE LOG CABIN

C 1900

Maker unknown. United States.

Multicolored silks and velvets, mainly black with bright colors; pink silk border with pink eyelet edging. Some shattering of silk fabrics.

$600-$750

PINEAPPLE LOG CABIN COVERLET

C 1880

Maker unknown. United States.

Cotton plaids with red centers; two corners cut out to fit a four-poster bed. Red cotton back; back-to-front self-binding.

$600-$750

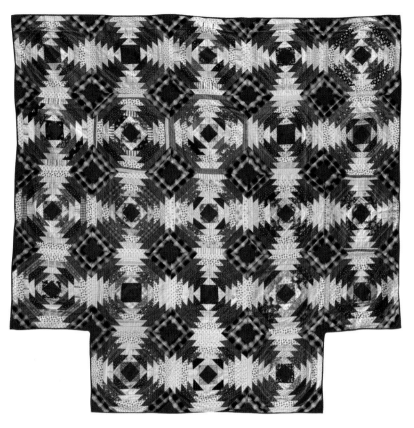

PINEAPPLE LOG CABIN TOP

C 1875

Maker unknown. United States.

Cotton stripes, checks, and microprints for lights, mainly blues, grays, reds, black-and-whites; brown madder floral cottons for darks; Turkey red cotton centers; hand pieced on muslin foundations, machine assembled.

$600-$750

HEXAGON LOG CABIN

C 1890

Maker unknown. United States.

Multicolored silks for logs; black silk triangles for centers. Black silk border.

$400-$600

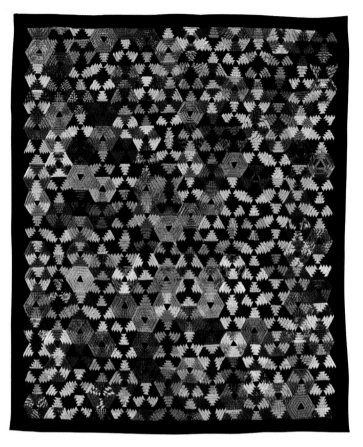

LOG CABIN THROW ON POINT

C 1935

Maker unknown. United States.

Multicolored silks, many probably from neckties; pink satin centers; blocks worked on the diagonal; decorative stitching. No batting. Pink satin back; back-to-front self-binding. Tied with pink floss.

$250-$400

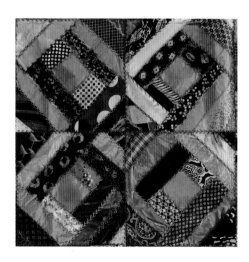

One-patch

One-patch designs, also known as mosaic patterns, are generally made from a single, usually geometric, shape. Pieces are combined with strong color contrasts. Often they create intricate three-dimensional patterns similar to designs found in ancient Greece, Rome and the Mideast.

SQUARES AND RECTANGLES

Patterns made from squares are among the simplest shapes to sew, and are found in numerous types of quilts. Examples from the late 1800s are often decorated or outlined with embroidery not dissimilar from the embroidery found on Crazy quilts from the same era. Fabrics were often heavier than the cottons that are normally used for quiltmaking, including wool and velvet.

DIAMONDS AND TRIANGLES

Triangles come in various forms, from irregular in which none of the sides are the same length, to isosceles in which two side are the same. However, the most common triangle found in one-patch quilts is the equilateral version, in which the sides and the angles are all equal. The true diamond, as distinct from the square turned on point, is found most often in Tumbling Blocks, also called Baby Blocks, and variations of Lone Star designs. Nineteenth-century examples are often made of fine fabrics like silk, velvet and satin, and cotton was also widely used.

HEXAGONS

By far the most familiar pattern using hexagons is Grandmother's Flower Garden and its numerous variations. The hexagon was widely used in British quilts beginning in the early 19th century in a pattern generally known as Honeycomb, but the familiar American version enjoyed its heyday in the 1920s and '30s, and numerous examples from that time period can be found.

Almost all Grandmother's Flower Garden quilts were made of cotton in bright or pastel colors, often solids, but many makers used prints, which they fussy-cut to create special effects. The central hexagon in each rosette is usually the same color, and the edges often follow the shape of the hexagon patches.

Both hexagons and diamonds are traditionally worked by cutting a paper template and a slightly larger fabric shape, which is then basted to the paper and stitched to its next-door neighbor. Because the papers are generally left in the piece until the top is completed, examples of unfinished tops can help in dating the work and its fabrics.

FOLDED

Quilts made from folded shapes are less popular than many other types, but the techniques make for fascinating visual effects. They are constructed from single units and are included in the One-patch section because they are handled in similar ways.

Yo-yos are circles of fabric gathered around the edge with a length of thread that is pulled tight, creating a smaller circle. These circles are then joined with a few stitches in rows, which are joined in the same way until the desired size is reached to make a coverlet rather than a batted quilt. There is usually no backing, and although the look is light and airy, the sheer volume of fabric means that bed-size pieces can be quite heavy. Their weight and construction method mean that they are fragile and need to be handled with care.

Cathedral Window, also called Mayflower, is a technique in which large squares of fabric, usually muslin, are folded into smaller squares and joined to make an all-in-one top and backing. The edges of the muslin squares are folded to enclose the raw edges of small squares of contrasting fabric and slipstitched in place to make a design that resembles a stained glass window. Both techniques are traditionally worked by hand and were popular in the 1930s.

AMISH SUNSHINE AND SHADOW

C 1935

Maker unknown, possibly a Mrs Stolfusz: initialed "A" on one back corner. Lancaster County, Pennsylvania.. Red, green, black, orange, purple, and pink cottons: squares set on point in concentric squares of color; wide burgundy cretonne border; plum corners; typical Lancaster Amish layout. Blue and white cotton check back; burgundy binding. Hand quilted cross hatch center, rose vine in border; typical Amish style.

$2,000-$3,000

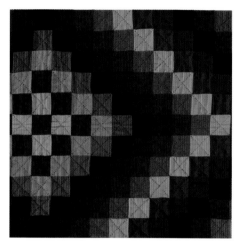

BISCUIT QUILT

C 1880

Maker unknown. Maine.

Multicolored silk squares separately padded; embellished between each square. Some repair to shattered squares using vintage silks. Silk print border.

$750-$1,000

CHECKERBOARD QUILT

C 1900

Maker unknown. Nebraska.

Wool rectangles, possibly suiting samples, mainly alternating light and dark; brown wool border on three sides, light-colored pieced edge on the fourth side. Blanket batting. Striped wool back; knife-edge binding. Tied with red yarn.

$100-$250

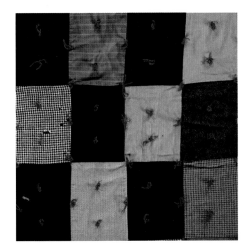

CHECKERBOARD SQUARES TOP

C 1910

Maker unknown. United States.

Japanese-style cotton prints: central section fuchsia and brown, two rows at one end, three rows at the other, blue and yellow floral; blue cotton print spacers, some pieced.

$100-$250

Chapter 2: Patchwork Quilts

TUMBLING BLOCKS

C 1875 (top)

Maker unknown. Quilted by Carol Brown, 2002. Multicolored 19th-century cotton prints and solids; hand pieced; new brown cotton print border. New brown on cream cotton microprint back; brown print binding. Machine quilted.

$600-$750

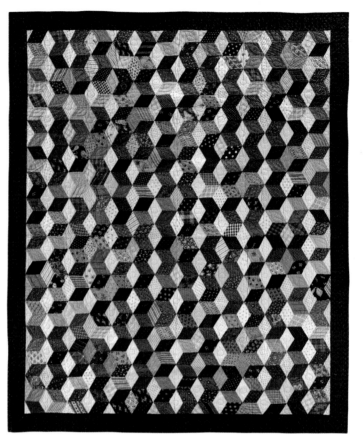

TUMBLING BLOCKS TOP

After 1880

Maker unknown. United States, probably New England.

Multicolored silk scraps; brown velvet, mitered border, possibly added later. Hand pieced using the English paper-piecing method, including paper templates cut from old school records papers dated "188__."

$400-$600

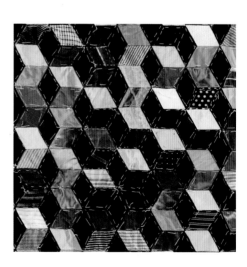

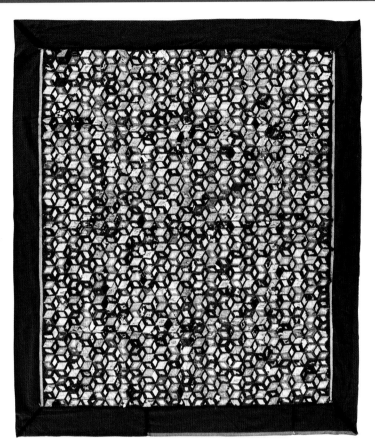

TUMBLING BLOCKS TOP

After 1880

Maker unknown. United States, probably New England.

Multicolored silk scraps; brown velvet, mitered border, possibly added later. Hand pieced using the English paper-piecing method, including paper templates cut from old school records papers dated "188__."

$400-$600

TUMBLING BLOCKS TOP

C 1935

Maker unknown. United States.

Yellow, orange and gold cotton sateen diamonds, triple border; hand pieced, possibly from a kit, possibly by Hubert Ver Mehren, founder of Home Art Studios.

$250-$400

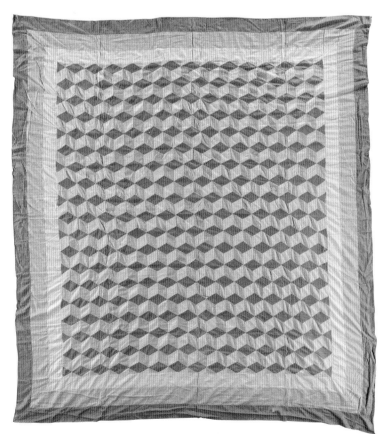

TUMBLING BLOCKS

C 1900

Maker unknown. United States.

Multicolored wool scraps, predominantly blacks and pinks; each diamond outlined in feather stitch; black wool border. Flannel or thin blanket batting. Plaid wool back; back-to-front self-binding. Tied.

$400-$600

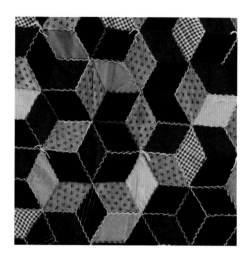

TUMBLING BLOCKS TOP

C 1940

Maker unknown. United States.

Pastel cotton prints and solids assembled roughly in vertical rows; machine pieced.

$100 or less

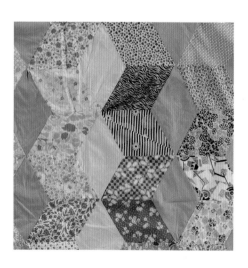

CHEVRON TOP

C 1880

Maker unknown. United States.

Multicolored cotton solids, prints, stripes, plaids and checks assembled in vertical rows of mainly light and dark. Hand pieced.

$100-$250

HEXAGON STAR BABY BLOCKS THROW

C 1930

Maker unknown. United States.

Multicolored silks, rayons, cotton sateens, taffeta and moires assembled into hexagon stars; black silk spacers; pieced border again using hexagon stars. Cotton batting. Black rayon back; wide back-to-front self-binding, edges covered by edges of the pieced border. Outline quilting.

$500-$750

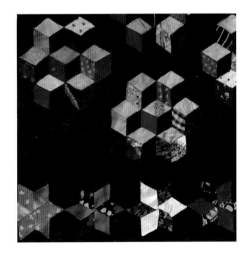

1,000 PYRAMIDS

C 1875

Maker unknown. Pennsylvania.

Multicolored cotton solids, prints, stripes, plaids and checks; almost a charm quilt but with a few repeated fabrics; some triangles pieced. Green, black and orange print back; and over-dyed green binding.

$1,750-$2,000

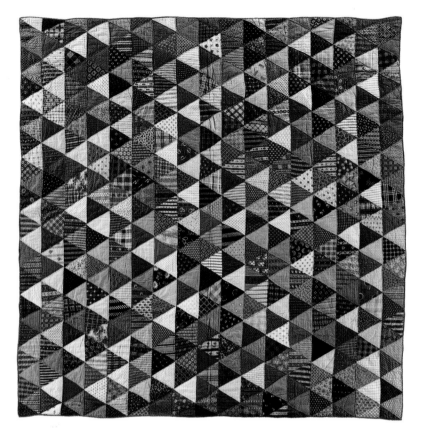

1,000 PYRAMIDS TOP

C 1900

Maker a member of the McBride family. Cedarburg, Wisconsin.

Multicolored cotton shirtings: prints, plaids, stripes, checks and solids; hand pieced.

$100-$250

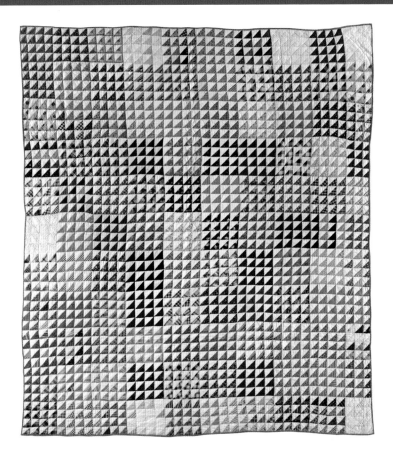

TILE MOSAIC
C 1880

Maker unknown. United States.

Multicolored cotton shirtings and scraps assembled as 16-patch blocks from half-square triangles; 3,344 pieces. Cotton print back, uneven brown and tan stripe with a red-orange motif; blue-and-white-striped binding.

$500–$750

GRANDMOTHER'S FLOWER GARDEN
C 1930

Maker unknown. United States.

Multicolored cotton prints and solids with white cotton "paths;" multicolored pieced edge of hexagons. White cotton back; knife-edge binding. Beautifully hand-quilted outline.

$250–$400

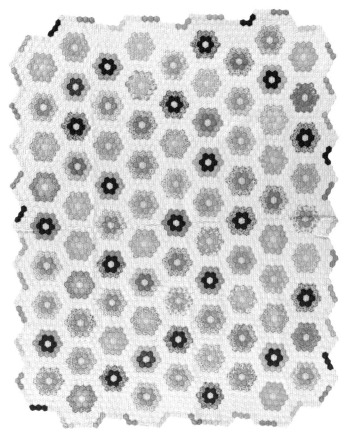

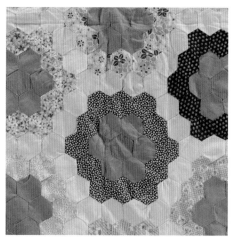

GRANDMOTHER'S FLOWER GARDEN TOP

C 1930

Maker unknown. Ohio.

Multicolored cotton solids with orange centers and purple inner rows; white "paths;" hand pieced.

$100 or less

GRANDMOTHER'S FLOWER GARDEN

Probably 1934

Maker likely Nora O. Adams of Enfield, Ill. Made from dressmaking scraps from friends of Nora Adams in North Liberty, Ind. Bartered for lessons and books given by Elizabeth Towne, grandmother of the owner, as per a letter dated April 17, 1935.

Multicolored cotton prints and solids with white "paths;" white hexagon border, straight on top and bottom edges, following shape of blocks on two opposite sides. White cotton back; knife edge binding.

$300-$500

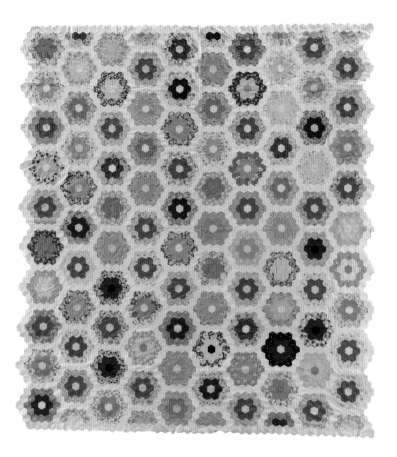

GRANDMOTHER'S FLOWER GARDEN COVERLET

C 1900

Maker unknown. Britain.

Multicolored cotton prints and solids set as "Trip Around the World;" white cotton "paths." No batting. Appliquéd to a blue cotton sheet following the edges of the blocks. No quilting.

$250–$400

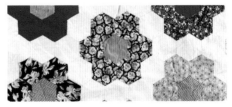

GRANDMOTHER'S FLOWER GARDEN

C 1925

Maker unknown. United States.

Multicolored cotton prints and solids with white "paths" and pink diamond "stepping stones." Muslin back; knife-edge binding following shapes of the blocks.

$250-$400

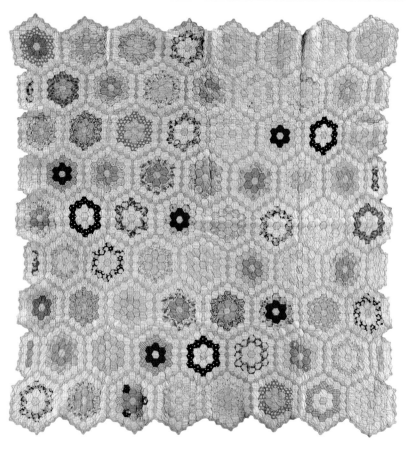

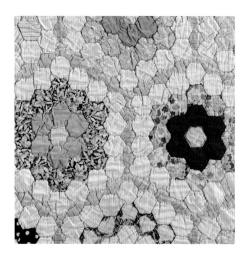

GRANDMOTHER'S FLOWER GARDEN

Pre-1924

Maker Aletta Belle Anderson Stephenson of Mason City, Iowa, grandmother of the owner.

Multicolored cotton prints and solids with green "paths;" green borders of pieced hexagons, top and bottom edges straight, opposite sides following the shape of the blocks. Green back; knife-edge binding.

$400-$600

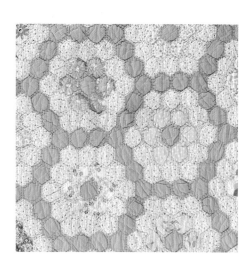

GRANDMOTHER'S FLOWER GARDEN TOP

20th century
Maker unknown. United States.
Multicolored cotton prints and solids; hexagons arranged in lozenge shape; light green outer band, darker green "paths;" hand pieced.
$100-$250

GRANDMOTHER'S FLOWER GARDEN

C 1875
Maker unknown. United States.
Multicolored cotton prints and solids in lozenge shapes; random configuration of hexagons except in one block; white cotton "paths;" red and white triangle pieced border, possibly added later. Cotton batting. Homespun back; red binding. Some wear.
$400-$600

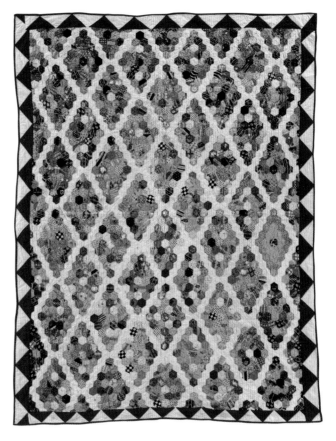

GRANDMOTHER'S FLOWER GARDEN
C 1930
Maker unknown. United States.
Multicolored cotton prints and solids; hexagons arranged in lozenge shapes; pink cotton double "path." Cream cotton back; cream binding.
$400-$600

HEXAGON TRIP AROUND THE WORLD
C 1925
Maker unknown. United States.
Multicolored cotton solids and prints, predominantly red. Thick batting. Muslin back; back-to-front self-binding. Hand quilted outline.
$250-$400

YO-YO COVERLET

C 1935

Maker unknown. United States.

Multicolored cotton prints; purple cotton "sash;" two opposite sides straight, two sides with points of yo-yos. No back.

$600-$750

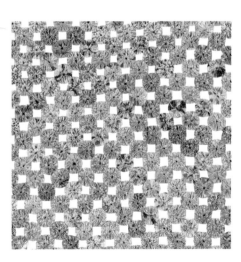

PASTEL YO-YO MEDALLION COVERLET

C 1930

Maker unknown. United States.

Cotton dress and apron scraps, mainly prints, greens, yellows, purples and blues; central diamond, mainly orange and green cotton solids; zigzag edge on three sides made from yo-yos. Large size; good design; excellent condition.

$400-$600

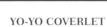

YO-YO COVERLET

C 1940

Maker unknown. United States.
Multicolored cotton prints, solids, stripes and plaids; random arrangement with some patterns evident; yo-yos sewn edge to edge. No batting. Pink sateen back; knife-edge binding.

$400-$600

CATHEDRAL WINDOW COVERLET

C 1960

Maker unknown. Greenwood, Miss.
Multicolored cotton scraps in muslin "windows." Self backed and bound.

$250-$400

Traditional Blocks

Block patchwork is regarded as an American invention, and it is certainly the most familiar style of quilt for most people. Blocks were a part of the pioneer tradition, and an enormous variety of vintage block quilts are still found throughout the United States, carried to the farthest reaches of the country as settlement moved westward.

Blocks are generally based on geometric principles, starting with simple squares or rectangles and dividing them into smaller units. Half-square triangles are widely used and their diagonal lines create interesting shapes that are lively and delineate one pattern from another. By the middle of the 19th century, most quilts were made of cotton, though wool and homespun were also used.

As techniques for dyeing developed and colorfastness was the norm rather than a lucky phenomenon, colors became brighter, but with the Colonial Revival period in the early 20th century came pastels. Colors brightened again during the Great Depression of the 1930s, when spirits needed a lift and quiltmakers made use of everything from printed feedsacks to scraps from dressmaking to reusable parts of worn-out clothes and household textiles.

The variety of block quilts is limitless, and myriad examples exist.

FOUR-PATCH

Like the nine-patch block, the four patch is simple and easy to construct, but its variations make it extremely versatile. With two sets of contrasting squares alternating, its potential for variety is mathematically smaller than that of the nine patch, but there are still enough four-patch patterns to have kept quiltmakers busy for at least 200 years.

As with nine-patch quilts, the simple examples are not usually considered valuable, but the more complex versions can command attention and higher prices.

PINWHEEL

Pinwheel is probably the best-known and most widely worked four-patch variation. In its simplest form, it consists of four identical squares constructed from two contrasting half-square triangles that are then combined to create a spinning effect. It is also called variously Windmill, Waterwheel or Millwheel. As with most simple blocks, there are myriad variations of the pattern, and age and complexity are the main factors that add value. Though most Pinwheel quilts are made from cotton, because the block is simple to construct, wool versions can also be found.

FLYFOOT

Another fascinating four-patch block is Flyfoot. The pattern has seldom been made since the 1940s, because its other name is Swastika. The motif, however, is an ancient symbol shaped as a cross in which the end of each arm is bent at a right angle. It has existed for millennia as a religious insignia among Hindus and Buddhists, and found inscribed in archaeological remains in pre-Columbian North and South America.

The Greeks, Celts and Byzantines all used the motif. Its well-known link to Nazism in Hitler's Germany has ended its popularity, but this means that Flyfoot quilts are almost all pre-1939, and its relative rarity can add value.

BOWTIE

The bowtie block is constructed of squares and triangles. Most of the examples I have run across are made from scraps.

FIVE-PATCH

The five-patch block is found less often than four patch or nine patch, but it forms the basis for many traditional patterns. It is made from five rows of five squares each. The Courthouse Square, or Album block, is a five-patch variation.

NINE-PATCH

The basic nine-patch block is made from nine squares arranged in three rows of three. The simplest version has squares of contrasting colors alternating to give a checkerboard effect, but once you begin to divide the squares into smaller squares, rectangles, triangles or diamonds, the variations become practically limitless. Many familiar and lesser-known patchwork patterns are based on the nine-patch arrangement.

Simple nine-patch quilts are charming, but unless they are particularly old, contain many rare fabrics or display exquisite workmanship, they are generally less valuable than the more intricate variations.

JACOB'S LADDER

Jacob's Ladder is a nine-patch variation block that comes in many variations. It consists of five four-patch squares that alternate with four squares each constructed from two half-square triangles. The choice of colors creates the diagonal ladder effect. Pioneers gave biblical names to many familiar patchwork block patterns, which reflects the religious nature of their daily lives, and Jacob's Ladder was a popular design across the heartland of America during the mid-to-late 19th century.

CHAINS

The most familiar chain pattern is Irish Chain, which has numerous variations. The simplest version is Single Irish Chain, which is often based on strategically placed nine-patch blocks; the most complex is Triple Irish Chain, in which several rows of squares create an intricate pattern of colored squares. In between is Double Irish Chain, which is the most common version. The setting squares are sometimes pieced or appliquéd, but normally the large blank spaces between the chains contain quilted motifs.

OCEAN WAVES

This pattern was popular in the late 1800s and is often made in blue and white. Blue and white were the colors of the Women's Christian Temperance Union, an anti-alcohol movement whose members, mainly female, made thousands of quilts in these colors.

COMPLEX BLOCKS

Some quilt block patterns are hard to categorize. Many of them are variations of less-complicated patterns, and they share the fact that their construction is not always straightforward. However, they create interesting and beautiful designs that repay any difficulty involved in making them.

SQUARE IN A SQUARE TOP

C 1890

Maker unknown. United States.

Cotton shirtings, solids and prints for blocks, predominantly browns; double pink sashing with hourglass corners; hand pieced.

$100-$250

SQUARE IN A SQUARE CROSS

C 1890

Maker unknown. United States.

Multicolored cotton prints and solids, including many shirtings, for blocks set on point in rows; acid yellow zigzag sashing. Red and white swastika print cotton back; back-to-front self-binding. Hand quilted.

$600-$750

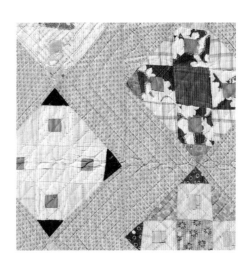

BOY'S NONSENSE TOP

C 1890
Maker unknown. United States.
Cotton shirtings, mainly blue, gray and white; double
pink spacers, some pieced; no corner triangles;
machine pieced.

$100-$250

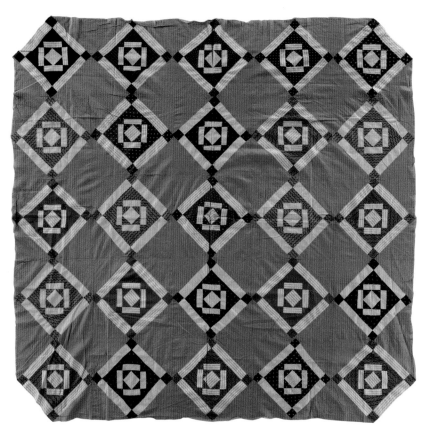

ALBUM BLOCK

20th century
Maker unknown. Missouri.
Pink-and-white cotton solids; white cotton ice cream
cone border with scalloped edge. Muslin back; pink
cotton binding. Hand quilted, pencil marking still
visible. Unwashed.

$250-$400

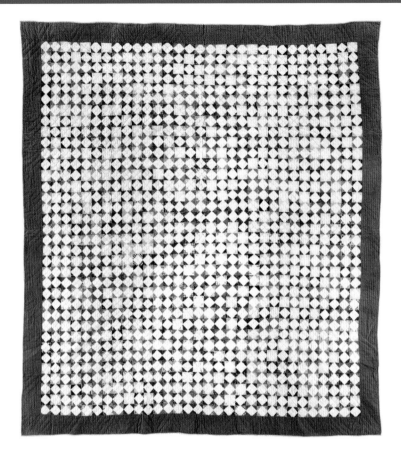

CONFETTI

C 1880

Maker unknown. United States.

Multicolored cotton scraps, white cotton centers, reddish-brown cotton print border. Muslin back; back-to-front self-binding. Hand-quilted crosshatch.

$750-$1,000

FOUR-PATCH TOP

C 1880

Maker unknown. United States.

Multicolored cotton prints and solids, blues, reds, blacks and whites, many shirtings; orange cotton print spacers. Hand pieced.

$100-$250

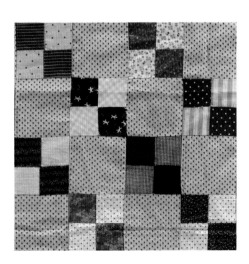

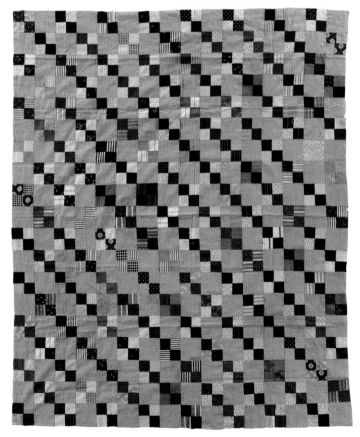

HOURGLASS VARIATION

C 1950

Maker unknown. Probably Missouri.
Multicolored cotton prints and solids; yellow cotton
spacers. Blue cotton back; back-to-front self-binding.
Hand-quilted outline in blocks, parallel diagonal lines
in spacers.

$250-$400

DOUBLE-T

C 1890

Maker unknown. Kansas.
Blue and white cotton microprint (five-point star)
with white cotton backgrounds; white/blue/white
cottons, triple border. White cotton back; blue
microprint binding. Hand quilted outline and grid;
parallel lines in borders.

$750-$1,000

RED CROSSES TOP

C 1900

Maker unknown. United States.

Red cotton solids and prints; indigo prints, including two different micro stars. Red cotton sashing and border. Hand pieced.

$100-$250

DOUBLE-SIDED CROSSROADS

C 1840

Maker unknown. United States.

Pre-Civil War cotton prints and solids, tan, black, and pink; back (not shown) is Courthouse Square in similar colors with tan sashing and chrome yellow corners. Wool batting. Hand quilted. Very worn.

$750-$1,000

RAILROAD CROSSING

C 1910 (top)

Maker unknown (top). Quilted by Patricia Cox, 2007. Edina, Minnesota.

Multicolored cotton prints and solids, mainly small scraps for miniature Railroad Crossing blocks. Feedsack sashing and border. New muslin back; new binding. Hand-quilted parallel lines.

$400-$600

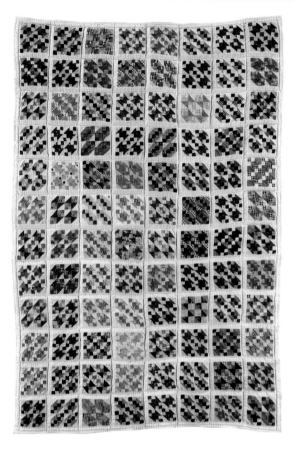

PINWHEEL

C 1880 (top). Quilted 2002.

Maker unknown. United States.

A variety of blue and white microprints and solids with white; new blue print border. New blue and white back; matching binding. New machine quilting.

$400-$600

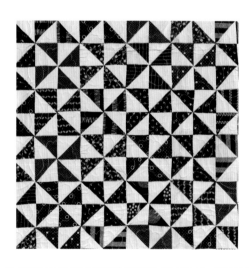

PINWHEEL

20th century

Maker unknown. United States.

Red and white cotton solids with a section restored with solid white; white cotton border. White cotton back; knife-edge binding.

$100-$250

WHIRLIGIG PINWHEEL

C 1870

Maker unknown. Missouri.

Gray and white cotton prints and stripes; double pink spacers; brown and red print inner border, double pink outer border. Dark-brown print back; matching binding. Hand-quilted crosshatch. Unwashed and unused.

$750-$1,000

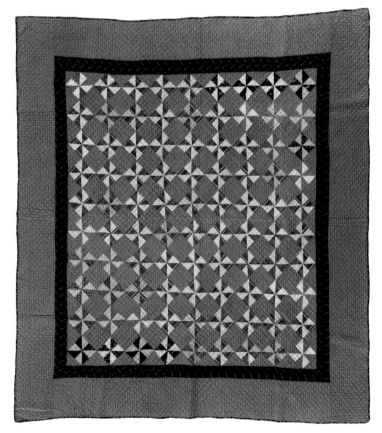

PINWHEEL

C 1925

Maker unknown. United States.

Pale pastel floral microprints on muslin background; pale mauve inner border, muslin outer border. Muslin back; knife-edge binding. Hand-quilted crosshatch and grid.

$100-$250

PINWHEEL STARS TOP

C 1910

Maker unknown. United States.

Multicolored cotton prints and solids, including shirtings, mourning prints, ginghams, indigos; bright-blue cotton sashing.

$100-$250

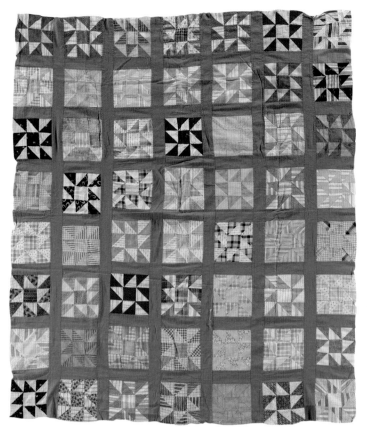

FOUR-PATCH PINWHEEL

C 1900

Maker: Melissa Belle Boucher (1868-1959), grandmother of the owner. Grantsville, Maryland. Colored cotton shirtings, muslin backgrounds and spacers; triple border. Muslin back; knife-edge quilting.

$250-$400

PROPELLER VARIATION

Post 1950

Maker unknown. East Texas.

Cotton solids and prints, blue silky finish border. Light-blue cotton back, back-to-front self-binding.

$400-$600

FLYFOOT TOP

C 1900

Maker unknown. United States.

Cotton shirtings; burgundy setting squares; hand pieced.

$100-$250

VIRGINIA REEL COMFORTER

1930s-1960s

Maker of the top: Mary Langer Daubrawa, great-great-grandmother of the owner. Waterloo, Wis. Borders and back added by Ardis Daubrawa Walters, grandmother of the owner, and Virginia Lorence Walters, mother of the owner, in the 1960s. Blocks are cotton shirtings; cotton sashing. Later borders are lavender cotton. Cotton back, knife-edge binding. Tied as a comforter.

$100-$250

SWASTIKA

C 1923

Maker Ellen (Mrs. Eli) Knox. Cherry Valley, Illinois. Peach and cream cotton blocks; cream sashing and borders. Cream back; peach binding. Hand-quilted wineglass and double parallel lines.

$250-$400

BOWTIE

C 1925

Maker unknown. Midwestern United States. Cotton shirtings with white cotton spacers, mainly pink and blue with striped blocks around the edges; gray border (somewhat frayed).

$100-$250

HOURGLASS VARIATION

C 1950

Maker unknown. Probably Missouri.
Multicolored cotton prints and solids; yellow cotton spacers. Blue cotton back; back-to-front self-binding. Hand-quilted outline in blocks, parallel diagonal lines in spacers.

$250-$400

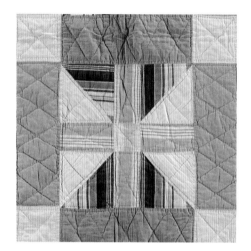

SCRAPPY BOWTIE

C 1950

Maker unknown. United States.
Multicolored cotton solids, prints, stripes, ginghams and plaids with muslin. Heavy cotton batting. White cotton back; back-to-front self-binding. Hand-quilted outline.

$250-$400

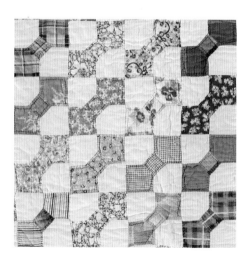

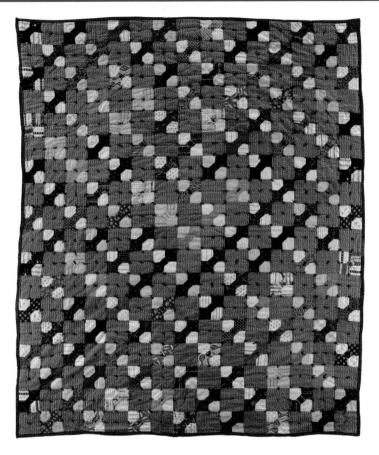

BOWTIE

C 1925

Maker Mary Peterson (1906-2001). Wisconsin.
Multicolored cotton prints and solids, many shirtings;
muslin; double pink cotton spacers. Thick batting.
Brown back; back-to-front self-binding. Tied with red
yarn.

$100-$250

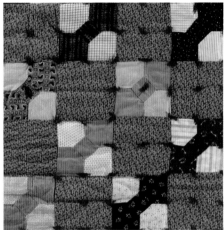

BOWTIE

C 1890 (top).
Maker unknown. Quilted by Jo Peterson circa 2000.
United States.
Cotton shirtings, many stripes, predominantly browns
and blues; cream microdot spacers; brown and cream
border. Blue and cream microprint back; brown
binding. Hand quilted in the ditch on blocks, floral
motif in spacers.

$400-$600

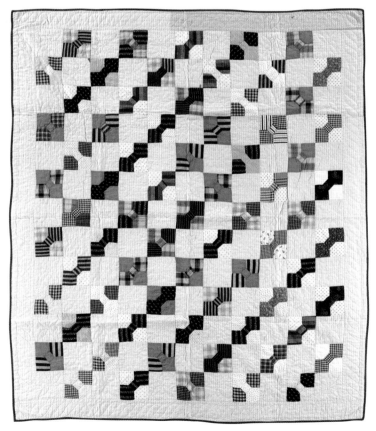

DIAGONAL BOWTIE

C 1900

Maker unknown. United States.

Cotton shirtings and prints; muslin; set diagonally.
Muslin back; back-to-front self-binding. Hand-quilted
curved lines.

$400-$600

BOWTIE

C 1900

Maker unknown. United States.

Cotton shirtings, mainly solids, checks, stripes; muslin.
Muslin back; print binding.

$250-$400

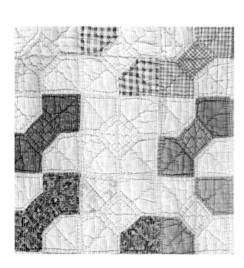

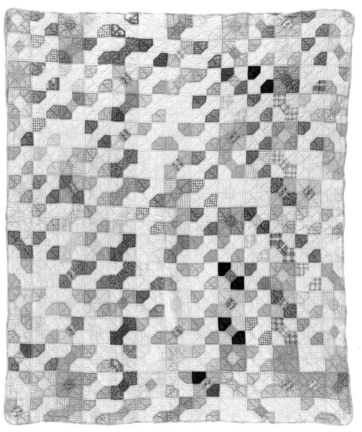

FIVE-PATCH TOP
20th century
Maker unknown. United States.
Multicolored cotton print shirtings, mainly checks and stripes with some small-scale prints; red and white cotton print spacers; blocks set on point.
$100-$250

MILLWHEEL (also called Single Wedding Ring and Crown of Thorns) TOP
C 1890
Maker unknown. United States.
Burgundy and cream cotton prints; burgundy cotton-print chevron sashing; 5"x5½" blocks; hand pieced.
$100-$250

CHIMNEY SWEEP TOP

C 1875

Maker unknown. United States.

Multicolored cotton prints and solids, predominantly green and white; white cotton sashing; white/green/ white cotton triple border, appliquéd corner squares; hand pieced.

$100-$250

COURTHOUSE SQUARE TOP

C 1900

Maker unknown. United States.

Multicolored cotton prints and solids, reds, blues, greens, browns with tan centers; gray cotton spacers. Hand pieced.

$100-$250

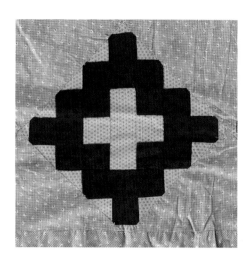

9-PATCH ON POINT TOP

C 1900

Maker unknown. United States.

Cotton shirtings, some double reds and indigos; red and white print chevron sashing; hand pieced.

$100 or less

9-PATCH ON POINT TOP

C 1900

Maker unknown. United States.

Cotton shirtings, some plaids, indigos, a few prints; red setting squares; machine pieced.

$100 or less

9-PATCH ON POINT TOP

C 1875

Maker unknown. United States.

Cotton shirtings assembled as a variation of H Block:
two rows X three squares with a central rectangle;
double pink setting squares; inner border green and
brown floral striped cotton, outer border double pink.

$100-$250

SASHED 9-PATCH TOP

C 1900

Maker unknown. United States.

A variety of 19th-century cotton fabrics; pieced
double pink sashing; blue and black striped border;
machine pieced.

$100-$250

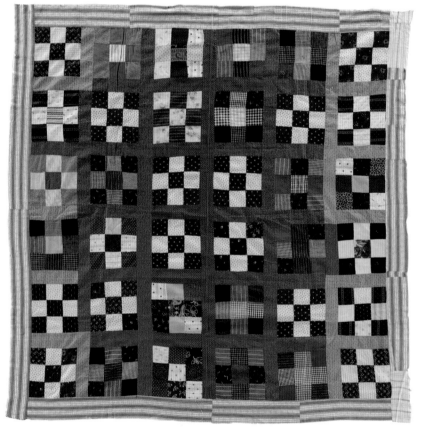

9-PATCH WITH RED SASHING

C 1890

Maker unknown. United States.

Cotton shirtings, many brown tones; red sashing. Red cotton print back; back-to-front self-binding with some fraying.

$250-$400

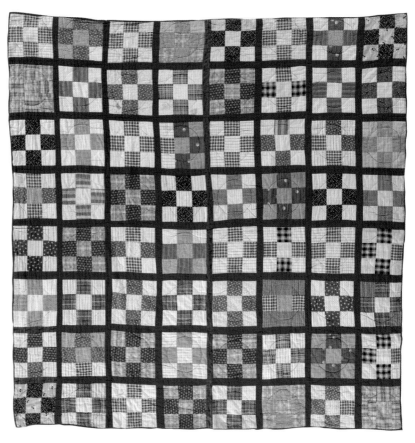

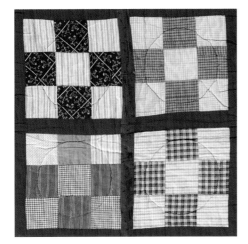

SILK 9-PATCH ON POINT COMFORTER

C 1900

Maker unknown. United States.

Multicolored silks embellished with multicolor feather stitch. Applied to a peachy-orange comforter.

$400-$600

9-PATCH ON POINT

C 1940

Maker Ellen McDermott Scott (1899-1972). Made for
Margaret Ellen Matthews Sankovitz (b. 1933), mother
of the owner. New Richmond, Wisconsin.
Various orange and white cottons, including some
cheddar; white border. Muslin back, white binding.
$100-$250

RED AND WHITE SHOOFLY

C 1935

Maker unknown. United States.
Red and white cotton prints and solids; hand-pieced
blocks; white cotton inner border, red cotton outer
border; machine assembly. White cotton back; white
binding. Hand-quilted hanging diamonds and
parallel diagonal lines.
$400-$600

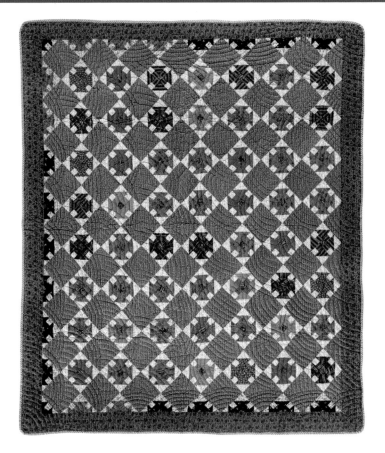

ANVIL ON POINT

C 1875

Maker unknown. United States.

Cotton shirtings, browns, paisleys, florals, double pinks; double pink setting squares; half-blocks on three sides; brown floral cotton print border. Cream muslin back; pale orange and red cotton print binding. Hand quilted fans. Unused; unwashed.

$1,000-$1,500

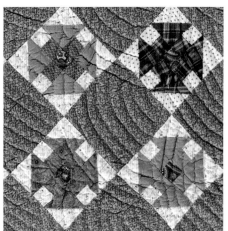

CHURN DASH IN DIAGONAL ROWS

C 1875

Maker unknown. United States.

Cotton shirtings; yellow and black cotton print setting squares. Yellow cotton back; yellow binding.

$400-$600

CHURN DASH ON POINT

C 1890

Maker unknown. United States.

Cotton prints and solids; red and white cotton print chevron sashing; narrow red and white cotton print border at top and bottom. Thin cotton batting. Red and cream cotton print back; red binding. Some staining and loss of fabric.

$250-$400

LETTER X 9-PATCH ON POINT

C 1900

Maker unknown. United States.

Cotton solids and prints, white, double pinks, cheddar and reds. White back; white binding.

$250-$400

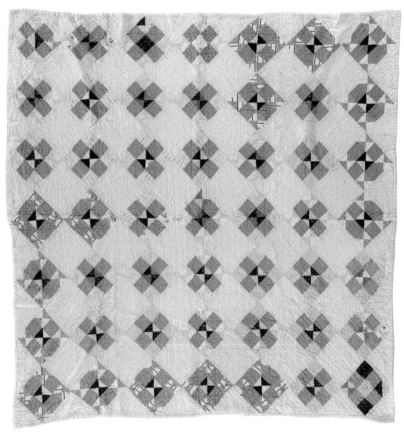

CAT'S CRADLE TOP

1930s

Maker unknown. United States.

Multicolored cotton scraps, white background; blocks hand pieced and set on point; yellow cotton chevron setting; machine assembly.

$100-$250

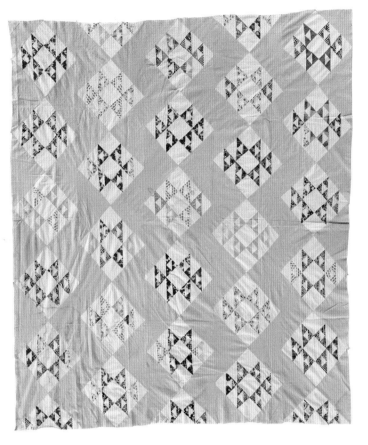

JACOB'S LADDER

1930s

Maker Ellen McDermott Scott (1899-1972). New Richmond, Wisconsin.

Cotton shirtings, mainly blues and pinks; muslin. Muslin back; new cream binding. Minimal quilting.

$100-$250

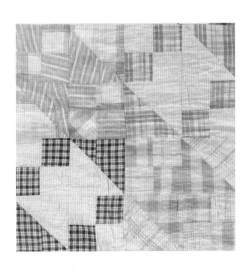

DOUBLE-SIDED JACOB'S LADDER

C 1890

Maker unknown. Texas or Tennessee.
Cotton and silk solids and prints; mainly Jacob's
Ladder blocks set in random directions, some
Checkerboard and other traditional blocks on top.
Back pieced in strips; back-to-front self-binding. Hand
quilted.

$250-$400

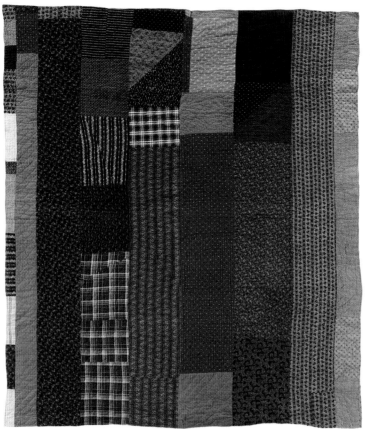

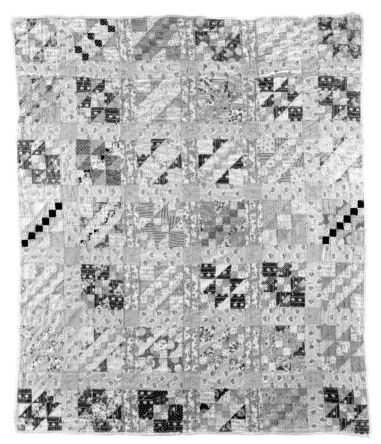

FEEDSACK JACOB'S LADDER

C 1935

Maker unknown. Texas.

Multicolored cotton feedsack prints and solids; two different turquoise prints for sashing, peach corner blocks. Back is pieced from feedsacks of the same design to appear as one overall piece; muslin binding. Thin batting. Tied with peach yarn.

$250-$400

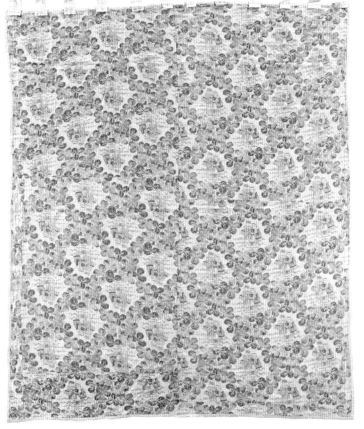

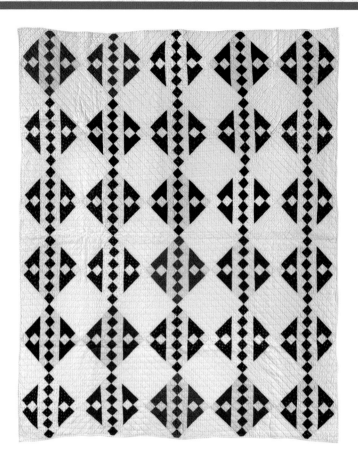

JACOB'S LADDER ON POINT

C 1900

Maker unknown. Iowa.

Blue cotton prints, pale cotton microdot spacers; set on point. Muslin back; red and white microdot binding. Hand-quilted grid.

$400-$600

SINGLE IRISH CHAIN

C 1900

Maker unknown. United States.

Burgundy and cream solids in nine-patch blocks set on point; muslin border. Muslin back; separate muslin binding. Hand-quilted crosshatch.

$100-$250

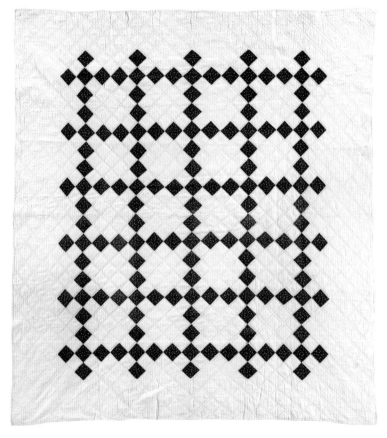

SINGLE IRISH CHAIN

C 1935

Maker unknown. United States.

Multicolored cotton prints and solids; chartreuse and cream cotton solids for nine-patch centers; cream cotton background. Cotton batting. Kelly green back; knife-edge binding sewn with big stitches. Simple hand quilting.

$250-$400

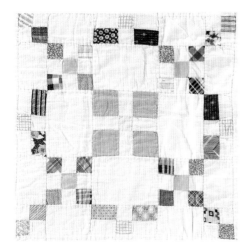

SINGLE IRISH CHAIN

C 1910

Maker unknown. United States.

Red and white chain print cotton in nine-patch blocks set square; muslin background, spacers and border. Muslin back; red cotton, scalloped binding. Elaborately hand quilted: crosshatch and wineglass on blocks, feather wreaths with dahlia centers in spacers; clamshell and cables on border.

$600-$750

SINGLE IRISH CHAIN TOP

C 1880

Maker unknown. United States.

Cotton prints and solids, predominantly indigos and blacks, with some mourning prints; nine-patch blocks set on point; red and white cotton prints including a horseshoe with whip conversation print for setting squares; hand pieced. Some staining.

$100-$250

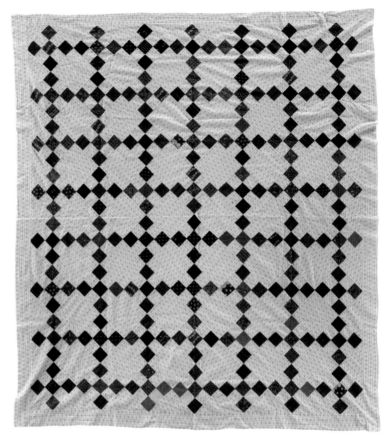

SINGLE IRISH CHAIN

C 1900

Maker unknown. United States.

Cotton prints and solids, predominantly blue, gray and red, assembled in four-patch/nine-patch blocks; blue cotton print sashing with various colors of four-patch corners; outer row of sashing creates border. Pieced binding.

$250-$400

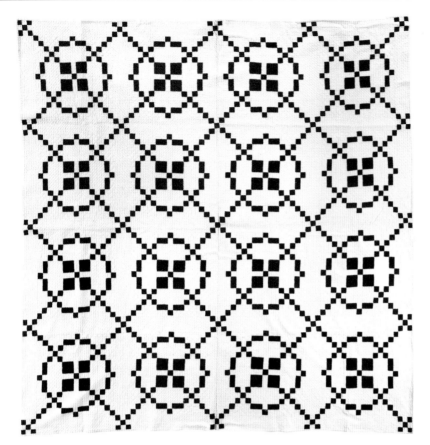

BURGOYNE SURROUNDED

C 1880

Maker unknown. United States.

Blue and white microprints on muslin background. Muslin back; muslin binding. Hand-quilted crosshatch.

$1,000-$1,500

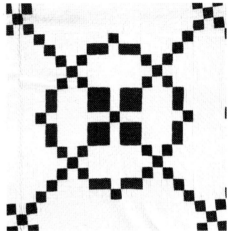

HOURGLASS CHAIN

C 1940

Maker: an aunt of the previous owner. Purchased by the present owner at a baseball game, where it was being used to wrap picnic equipment. Sturgeon Bay, Wisconsin.

Blue and white cotton solids. Cotton batting. White cotton back; separate white binding. Pattern is also known as a variation of Broken Dishes.

$400-$600

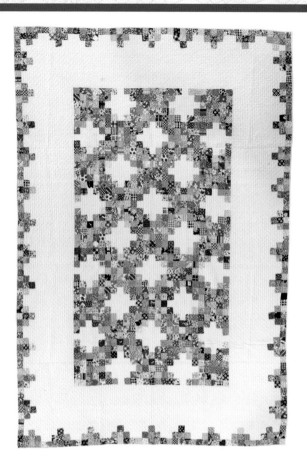

TRIPLE IRISH CHAIN
C 1950
Maker unknown. United States.
Multicolored cotton prints and solids; white spacers; blocks set square; pieced borders of white squares edged with multicolored squares arranged in steps. Cotton batting. White cotton back; white binding. Hand-quilted crosshatch.
$600-$750

DOUBLE IRISH CHAIN
1931
Maker Ellen McDermott Scott (1899-1972), New Richmond, Wis. Made as a gift for her daughter, Mary Terese McDermott (1901-1990), to celebrate her wedding on Aug. 10, 1931, to Richard J. Matthews, Sr., of Shorewood, Wisconsin.
Yellow and white cotton solids with blocks set on point; triple border of yellow/white/yellow with nine-patch corner squares. White cotton back; white cotton binding.
$400-$600

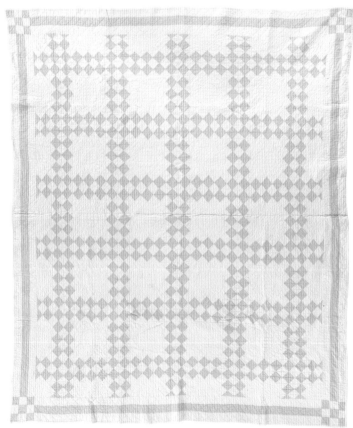

DOUBLE IRISH CHAIN

C 1930

Maker unknown. Germantown, Wisconsin.
Blue cotton solid chain; white cotton print
background; narrow white cotton border. Blue and
white print back; blue binding. Hand quilted.

$400-$600

DOUBLE IRISH CHAIN

C 1825 (top)

Maker unknown. Stamped on front: J.D.W. Randall.
Probably United States. Purchased as top, quilted by
Eileen Russell, Galena, Ohio, in 1999.
Multicolored cotton prints and solids; cream
background. New narrow cotton print border. New
muslin back; new gray binding. New hand quilting.

$2,000-$3,000

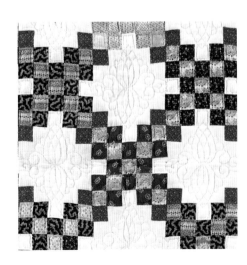

CHIPS AND WHETSTONES WITH DOUBLE IRISH CHAIN

C 1850

Maker unknown. Believed to have been made by a slave on a plantation near Pennington Gap, Virginia. Red, green and white cotton solids on white background for blocks; blue and white microdot cotton prints for chains. Cream back; blue microdot binding. Heavy hand quilting.

$2,000-$3,000

OCEAN WAVES

C 1880

Maker unknown. Indiana.

Various indigo cotton microdots, white cotton backgrounds and border. Muslin back; indigo cotton microdot binding. Hand-quilted outline, floral motif in centers, diagonal parallel lines on border.

$600-$750

OCEAN WAVES

C 1935

Maker unknown. United States.

Multicolored cotton prints and solids, mainly greens, blues, purples, grays and cream; green cotton inner border, cream cotton outer border. Muslin back; green cotton binding. Hand quilted.

$400-$600

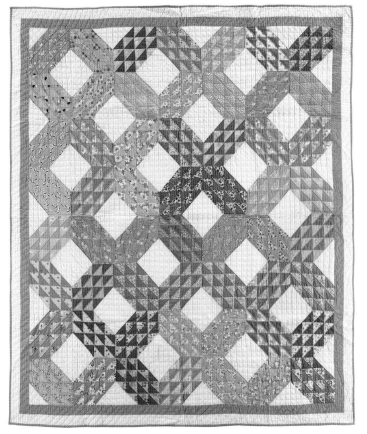

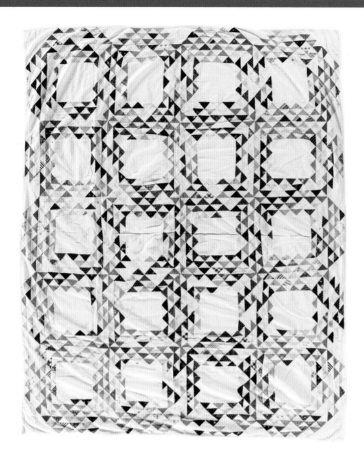

OCEAN WAVES TOP

C 1890

Maker unknown. United States.

Multicolored cotton scraps, mainly pinks, blues, browns and some conversation prints; muslin centers and setting triangles; machine pieced. Edge bound with muslin for stability. A few stains.

$100-$250

BEAR'S PAW

C 1890

Maker unknown. Wisconsin.

Multicolored cotton prints and solids, mainly shirtings, set on point; alternating with gray cotton spacers; multicolored pieced cotton diamonds border. Thin cotton batting. Print back (faded); back-to-front self-binding. Hand quilted.

$400-$600

WHEEL TOP

C 1900

Maker unknown. United States.

Multicolored cotton prints and solids, mainly blues, indigos, and black and whites. Pattern also known as Rolling Stone.

$100 or less

STORM AT SEA

C 1880

Maker unknown, initialed "H E" in one corner in chain stitch. United States.

Red, white and blue cotton prints and solids. Cream cotton back; blue cotton print binding on three sides, knife-edge on the fourth side. Hand-quilted outline and parallel lines.

$600-$750

BROKEN DISHES

C 1875 (top)

Maker unknown. Quilted by Carol Brown, Nashville, Tennessee.

Cotton prints and solids, mainly pinks, reds, blues, greens and grays; double pink sashing; new double red cotton border. New cotton print back; new double red print binding. Machine quilted.

$400-$600

WALLS OF JERICHO VARIATION

C 1940 (top)

Maker unknown. Quilted circa 1955. Ohio. Multicolored cotton prints and solids with consistent red corner squares in each block; white cotton spacers; all set on point; multicolored cotton pieced border of half-square triangles. White cotton back; white cotton binding. Hand-quilted outline on blocks, parallel lines on spacers.

$600-$750

DOVE IN THE WINDOW
C 1930 (top)

Maker unknown. Quilted by Jo Ann Peterson., circa 2000. United States.

Multicolored cotton print and solid scraps; white cotton backgrounds; blue cotton sashing with yellow cotton corners; new narrow yellow inner border, new blue-on-blue stripe cotton outer border. New blue floral back; blue striped cotton binding. Hand-quilted outline in blocks, cable in sashing, double crosshatch in blue border.

$750-$1,000

MOHAWK TRAIL
C 1945

Maker unknown. United States.

Multicolored cotton prints and solids, including stripes and chambrays, oranges, greens, reds, pinks and blues; cream backgrounds; multicolored pieced cotton border, on three sides, of fanlike blocks used in the main block. White cotton back; white cotton binding. Hand-quilted outline, eight-petaled floral motif in centers.

$400-$600

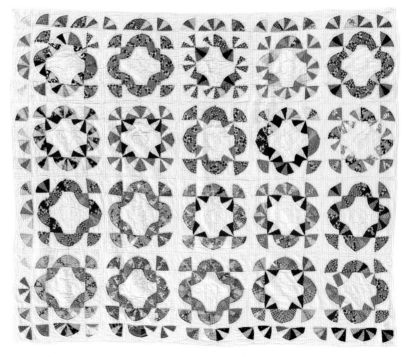

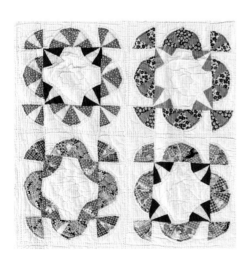

DELECTABLE MOUNTAINS

C 1880

Maker Marietta Pettit (1863-1940). Salem, Ohio. Blue cotton microprints and white cotton solids; blocks outlined in blue with white cotton spacers and set on point; white cotton border outlined inside and out with blue and white saw-tooth edges. White cotton back; narrow blue binding. Hand quilted feathered wreaths. Poor condition.

$100-$250

SAWTOOTH VARIATIONS TOP

C 1885

Maker unknown. United States.

White cotton solids; pieced sawtooth sashing in multicolored cotton scraps, including browns, pinks, grays, madders, some stripes and prints; corner squares at each intersection; multicolored Flying Geese pieced cotton border; hand pieced.

$400-$600

LOVER'S KNOT

C 1920

Maker unknown. United States.

Red and white cotton solids in interwoven strips; two red and white pieced side borders. Muslin back; white cotton binding. Hand-quilted outline and chevron.

$400-$600

CARPENTER'S SQUARE

C 1920

Maker Marietta Pettit (1863-1940). Salem, Ohio. Blue and white cotton solids; blue cotton inner border, white cotton outer border. White cotton back; blue cotton binding. Hand-quilted crosshatch and outline.

$400-$600

Representational Blocks

PLANTS

Floral patterns are common in appliqué, but there are also numerous pieced plant designs. Patchwork blocks depicting plant forms are generally very stylized.

BASKETS

Basket designs are among the most popular of pictorial, or representational, quilt patterns. There are baskets galore, including appliquéd versions, but most are based on geometric shapes, usually half-square triangles. Handles are often applied to the pieced block, and some patterns feature appliquéd flowers.

STARS

While there are more stars in the heavens than there are star patterns for quiltmaking, there are more variations of designs featuring stars than for any other motif. Stars with an even number of points—four, six or eight being the most numerous—lend themselves to piecing. Combining half-square triangles or diamonds is the most common way to achieve pieced stars, and even simple star quilts can be striking enough to carry a relatively high value.

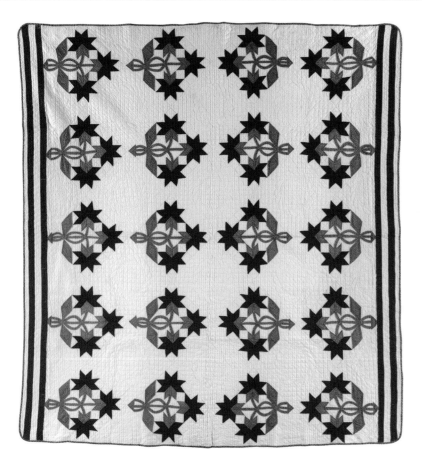

CAROLINA LILY

C 1850

Maker unknown. United States.

Solid red cotton flowers, green-on-cream cotton print stems and leaves, cream cotton background; hand pieced flowers and leaves with appliquéd stems; pieced border in four strips of red/cream/red/cream cotton solids on opposite sides. Cream cotton back; green print binding. Crosshatch and outline quilting.

$2,000-$3,000

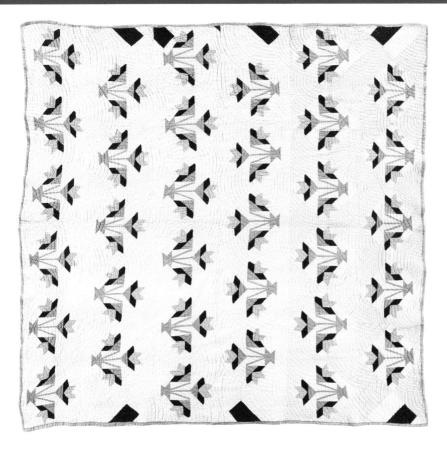

CAROLINA LILY

C 1900

Maker unknown. United States.

Cheddar orange and red cotton flowers; brown cotton baskets, leaves and stems, probably fugitive green; cream cotton background and spacers; red and cream bars on two opposite sides are later patches. Muslin back; pink cotton machine-applied binding. Fan quilting.

$250-$400

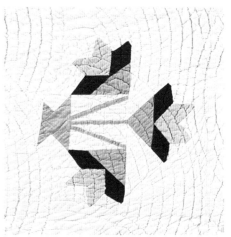

MOUNTAIN PINK

C 1940

Maker unknown. United States.

Multicolored cotton prints and solids on white background with grayish green block outlines; peach spacers. Thin cotton batting. Peach cotton back; green cotton binding. Outline quilting in pattern blocks; leaf motif in spacers.

$250-$400

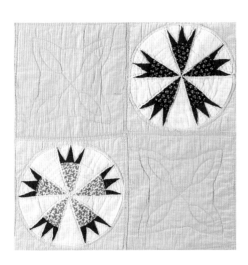

TREE OF LIFE

C 1875 (top)

Maker unknown. Quilted by Jo Peterson, 2004. United States.

Green and red cotton broadcloth tree trunks and leaves; white cotton backgrounds and spacers; triple border in blue-green, white and blue-green cotton. New back, new red binding. Hand quilted crosshatch grid; star motifs in spacers.

$1,000-$1,500

PINE TREE TOP

C 1900
Maker unknown. United States.
Cotton solids and prints; muslin background areas;
triple blue/white/blue borders on two opposite sides.
Hand pieced.

$100-$250

ENGLISH IVY

C 1875
Maker Opal Burrell. Part of the estate of Warren
Harding (not the U.S. president), Des Moines, Iowa.
Red cotton solids on cream cotton; hand pieced;
double border of red and white. Cream back; new
white binding. Hand-quilted crosshatch and double
lines.

$400-$600

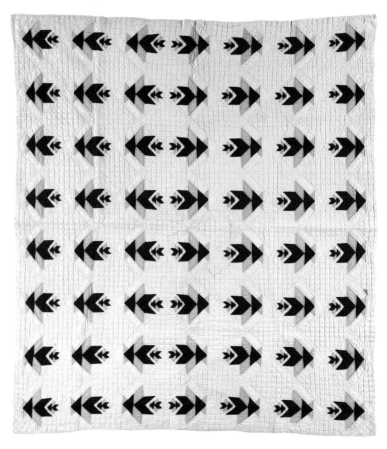

TEXAS CACTUS BASKET

C 1870

Maker unknown. United States.

Red and tan cotton solids; cream cotton background.
Cream cotton back; cream binding in several shades.
Hand-quilted crosshatch and outline.

$600–$750

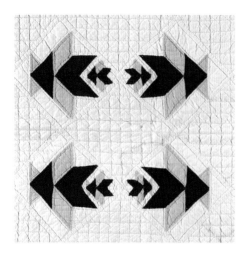

ROSE TRELLIS

C 1930

Maker unknown. United States. Possibly a pattern by
Anne Orr.

Pieced roses in pink, yellow, rose, purple and green cotton
solids on white cotton background; alternating with white
cotton spacer blocks; sashed "trellis" of blue cotton solid
with pink corners and corner triangles inside blocks; pieced
rose garland border of pink, rose and green cotton solids on
white background; blue cotton outer border. Muslin back;
pink binding. Hand-quilted flower motifs and crosshatch.

$200–$300

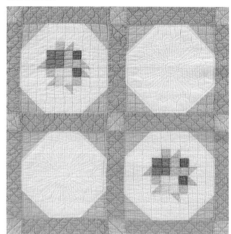

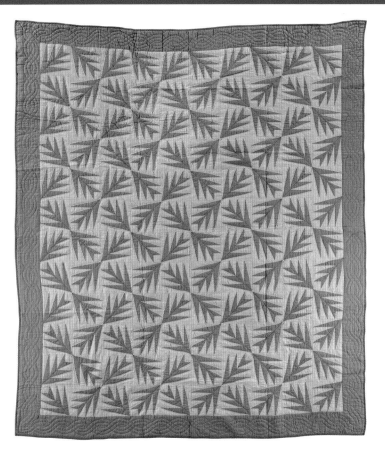

THE PALMS

C 1925 (top)

Maker: mother of Catherine Morrisey Gerster. Quilted by Jo Peterson, Superior, Wisconsin.

Green and tan cotton solids; green cotton border. New tan and pale orange cotton print back; new green binding. Hand quilted outline in blocks, cable in border.

$600-$750

COMPASS ROSE VARIATION

C 1915

Maker unknown. United States.

Multicolored scraps, predominantly green and yellow solids; green and white cotton double border; hand pieced. White cotton back; multicolored bias binding. Hand quilted outline in blocks, flower and leaf motifs in borders.

$250-$400

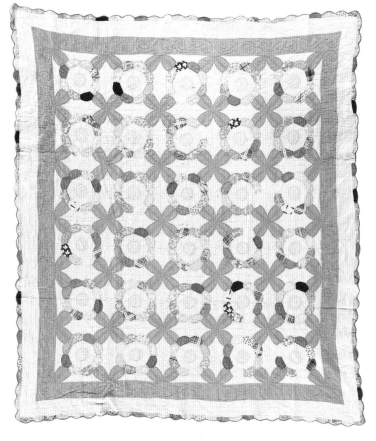

CHERRY BASKETS

C 1925

Maker unknown. United States, probably Wisconsin. Cotton print scraps, muslin background, red corner triangles; machine appliquéd bias handles; green sashing and border. Wool batting. Pink cotton back; back-to-front self-binding.

$400-$600

PIECED BASKETS TOP

C 1885

Maker unknown. United States. Multicolored cotton scraps and pink background; some baskets hand pieced, blocks machine pieced; blue dotted sashing with pink corners.

$100-$250

BASKET OF CHIPS

C 1915

Maker unknown. United States, probably Minnesota.
Dark-blue cotton baskets with pink calico and
shirting "chips;" light-blue cotton setting squares;
dark-blue cotton border with light-blue corners.
White back; blue binding. Hand-quilted crosshatch.

$400-$600

VARIABLE STAR

C 1865

Maker unknown. Frederick, Maryland.
Multicolored cotton prints with cream background
for star blocks, mainly reds, browns and greens, some
stripes; orange cotton print spacers. Muslin back;
double pink binding. Hand-quilted parallel lines in
star blocks, crosshatch on spacers.

$750-$1,000

DEVIL'S CLAW

C 1910

Maker unknown. United States, possibly Iowa.
Blue and white cotton solids; blocks set on point;
white cotton spacers. Purple cotton back; separate
purple binding. Hand-quilted crosshatch.

$750-$1,000

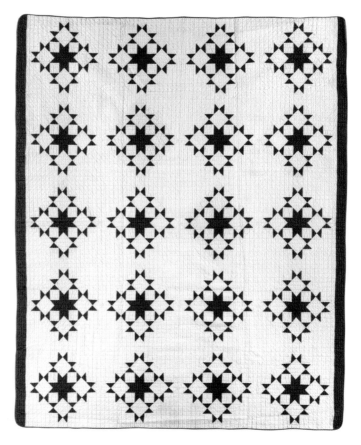

LIBERTY STAR

C 1920

Maker unknown. United States.

Red, white and blue strip-pieced cotton solids set on
point; white cotton spacers; pieced red, white and
blue cotton sashing; unusual set, perhaps unique.
White feedsack back; blue binding. Hand-quilted
outline, parallel lines and ditch quilting.

$750-$1,000

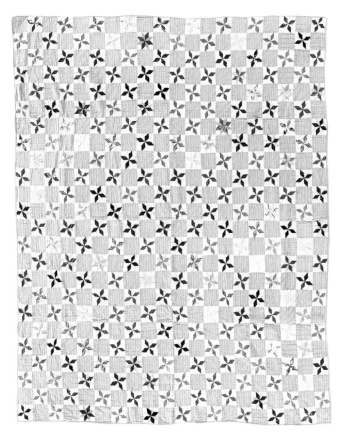

EIGHT-POINT MINI STARS

C 1880

Maker unknown. United States, probably Midwestern. Multicolored cotton prints and solids on white background for stars, some indigos, cadet blues, red/white and black/white prints, pink cotton spacers. Muslin back; pink cotton binding, frayed. Some wear. Hand quilted.

$100-$250

EIGHT-POINT STARS

C 1880

Maker unknown. British.

Indigo dotted blue cotton and muslin stars; pieced indigo and white diamond border. Muslin back: knife-edge binding. Hand quilted.

$250-$400

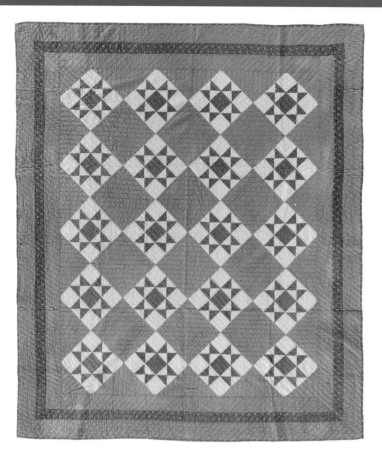

EIGHT-POINT OHIO STAR

C 1890

Maker unknown. United States.

Burgundy print and white cotton stars; purple microdot cotton spacers, possibly a fugitive color; burgundy print inner border, purple microdot outer border, mitered corners. Black and white checked cotton back; burgundy print binding. Hand quilted.

$200-$400

EIGHT-POINT SUNBURST STARS

C 1860

Maker unknown. Northern Wisconsin.

Multicolored cotton prints and solids with cream muslin on gray-blue background for pieced sunburst stars; double pink zigzag sashing; green cotton inner border (faded), double pink cotton outer border. Muslin back; double pink cotton binding. Hand quilted.

$750-$1,000

EIGHT-POINT SAWTOOTH SINGLE STAR

C 1835

Maker unknown. Palmyra County, Ohio.
Indigo microdot and white cotton stars, quite worn
with fading; narrow blue cotton inner border, wide
muslin inner border, narrow blue cotton outer border.
Muslin back; knife-edge binding. Grand prize winner
at Palmyra county fair 13 years in a row.

$750-$1,000

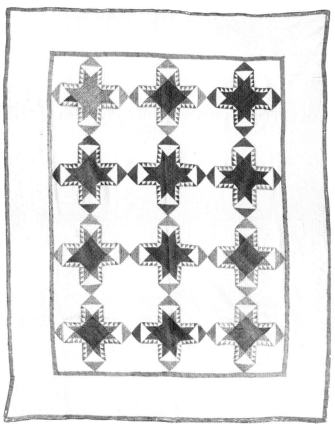

SINGLE STAR

C 1880

Maker unknown. United States.
Tan and cream cotton solids set on point; tan cotton
spacers; pieced bottom border; muslin beard guard
on top border. Muslin back; knife-edge binding.

$250-$400

PINWHEEL OHIO STAR

20th century

Maker unknown. United States.

Blue and white cotton solids for stars; white cotton sashing; blue and white half-square triangle pieced border on opposite sides. White cotton back; white cotton binding. Hand quilted.

$400-$600

LE MOYNE STARS

C 1930

Maker unknown. Probably a member of the Bowen family. Wisconsin.

Multicolored cotton prints and solids on white cotton background for stars; yellow cotton sashing; white cotton inner border, yellow cotton outer border. Yellow satin binding. Hand quilted.

$250-$400

EIGHT-POINT STAR NINE-PATCH

C 1900 (top).

Maker unknown, quilter unknown. Iowa.

Multicolored cotton print and solid scraps, white cotton backgrounds: five pieced stars and four plain squares per nine-patch block; pale orange cotton sashing with red cotton corner squares. Muslin back; back-to-front self-binding. Hand-quilted outline on stars, parallel lines on plain squares, cable in sashing.

$400-$600

EIGHT-POINT STARS

C 1900

Maker unknown. Illinois.

Multicolored cotton shirtings on white cotton backgrounds set on point; red/white setting squares and triangle border. Muslin back; back-to-front self-binding. Hand-quilted grid.

$400-$600

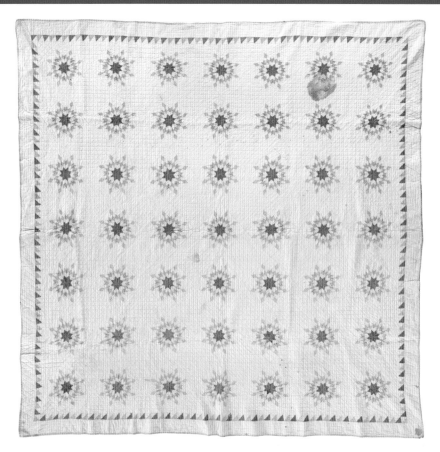

SNOWFLAKE STARS

C 1825

Maker unknown. United States.

Solid red centers, blue dotted snowflakes and points on white cotton backgrounds; saw-tooth inner border of alternating small half-square triangles blue/white or red/white, white outer border. White cotton back; blue binding very frayed. Some fading, some stains.

$700-$1,000

SEVEN SISTERS

C 1875 (top)

Maker unknown. Quilted by Jo Peterson, circa 2000. United States.

Red cotton print stars, tan floral cotton print background; green cotton setting triangles that create large secondary stars; new narrow red cotton inner border, new tan floral cotton print outer border; new tan cotton print back; new red binding. Hand quilted outline.

$750-$1,000

WHEEL OF FORTUNE (also called Lucky Star)

C 1920
Maker unknown. United States.
Green cotton centers, white cotton inner stars and star edges, multicolored cotton scraps for outer rings; green cotton setting diamonds; green cotton border. Green cotton back; darker green binding. Hand quilted.
$400-$600

MISSOURI MINI STARS

20th century
Maker unknown. United States, probably Midwest. Red and blue cotton six-point stars; blue and green cotton baby blocks as spacers. Aquamarine cotton back; red binding, straight on top and bottom, following diamond edge on opposite sides. Hand-quilted outline.
$400-$600

SIX-POINT STAR SOLDIER QUILT

C 1870

Maker unknown. British.

Brown and tan wool diamonds set as six-point stars with red wool diamond spacers: wool melton scraps from military uniforms. Heavy army blanket batting. Pieced wool back set as one large Courthouse Steps blocks. Brown wool binding. No quilting.

$600-$750

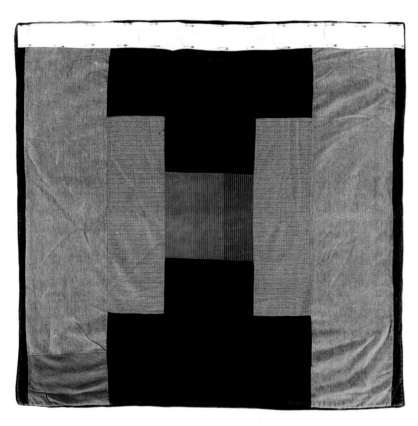

SIX-POINT STARS

C 1935

Maker unknown. Wisconsin.

Multicolored cotton prints and solids: diamonds set as six-point stars with green cotton diamond spacers. Green back; back-to-front self-binding. Hand quilted. Found in a dumpster and rescued by the present owner by climbing into the dumpster to retrieve it.

$100-$250

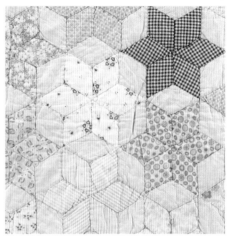

SIX-POINT STARS WITH HEXAGON CENTERS

1939

Maker Glenna Martin (at age 10), mother of the owner; quilted by Lottie Martin, grandmother of the owner (Lottie's mother).

Multicolored cotton prints and solids to make hexagon centers and star points; yellow cotton setting diamonds; some centers missing or faded. A blue dotted star has a white-on-white duck embroidered on it. Muslin back; white binding. Hand quilted.

$250-$400

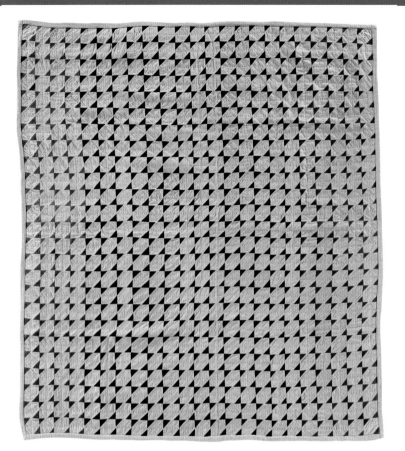

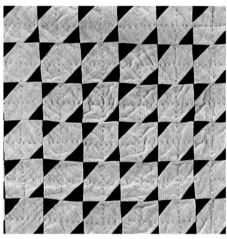

HEXAGON STARS

C 1890

Maker unknown. Nova Scotia, Canada.
Gray wool squares, many pieced, with two opposite
corners of dark blue wool set to create six-point stars.
Gray striped wool print back; gray binding. Hand-
quilted parallel lines.

$600-$750

SIX-POINT STARS TOP

C 1940

Maker unknown. United States.
Cotton prints and geometrics set as diamonds to
make six-point stars; apricot spacer hexagons; hand
pieced.

$100-$200

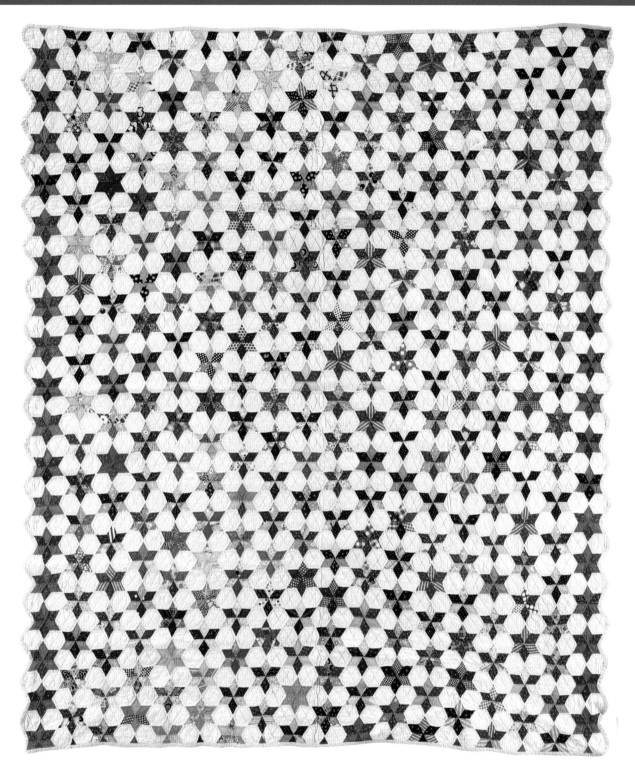

TOUCHING SIX-POINT STARS

C 1910

Maker unknown. United States.

Multicolored cotton prints including many indigo colors set to make six-point stars; white cotton spacer hexagons. Pink with white polka dot cotton back; pink binding. Hand quilted outline.

$750-$1,000

HEXAGON STARS TOP

C 1925

Maker unknown. United States.

Multicolored cotton prints and solids, including green, orange, cream, pink and tan, to make diamonds set as six-point stars set inside double hexagons; pink cotton setting triangles; pink cotton border. Machine pieced.

$100-$250

PONTIAC STARS

C 1910 (top)

Maker unknown. Quilted by Jo Peterson, 2004. United States.

Red and two shades of green, cotton four-point stars on cream, cotton backgrounds; a variety of cream, cotton spacers; new green inner and white outer cotton borders. New white, cotton back; new red, cotton binding. Elaborate motif hand quilting designed by Patricia Cox, Edina, Minn.

$600-$750

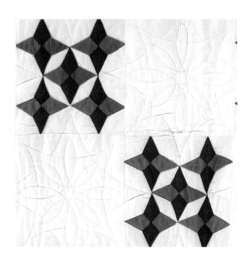

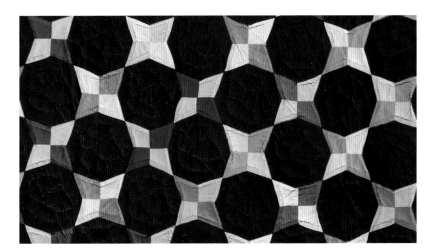

PERIWINKLE SNOWBALL

C 1960

Maker unknown, Midwestern Mennonite. United States.

Multicolored cotton solids to make four-point stars; black cotton eight-sided spacers; green cotton inner and black cotton outer borders. Blue cotton back; black cotton binding. Hand quilted outline on stars, three-lobed motif on spacers, cable and diamond cable on borders.

$400-$600

FOUR-BLOCK LONE STAR

C 1880

Maker unknown. United States, possibly Vermont. Red, cheddar, blue and tan cotton solids on tan cotton background; red cotton inner border, tan cotton outer border; stars hand pieced; blocks assembled by machine. Double pink stripe cotton back; red binding. Hand quilted.

$750-$1,000

STAR OF BETHLEHEM (also called Carpenter's Wheel)

C 1900

Maker unknown. United States.

Low contrast pastel cottons, including many shirtings and double pinks; pale yellow backgrounds; hand pieced. Black-and-white cotton striped print back; black and white binding with purple flowers. Hand quilted.

$250-$400

LONE STAR

C 1875

Maker unknown: professional Mennonite quiltmaker.
York, Pa.

Red, pinks, yellow, green and orange cotton solids
on bright, rose pink background; yellow/green/pink
mitered triple border. Striking double pink cotton
back; green cotton binding. Hand-quilted outline,
crosshatch and cables.

$1,500-$2,000

LONE STAR

C 1900

Maker unknown. Minnesota.

Pink, blue, green and mauve cotton solids on rose pink cotton background; rose pink and blue border of alternating pieced diamonds. Pink back; knife-edge quilting. Hand-quilted grid, crosshatch and outline.

$250-$400

LONE STAR

C 1930

Maker unknown. United States.

Orange, yellow and cream cotton solids on cream cotton background; pieced inner border of orange, yellow and cream diamonds, cream outer border. Muslin back; knife-edge binding. Hand-quilted outline and crosshatch. Some wear, particularly damage to binding on one edge.

$250-$400

GOLDEN LONE STAR

C 1925

Maker unknown. Iowa.

Various shades of yellow and orange cotton solids on white background; triple pieced border of gold triangles, yellow diamonds and orange ice cream cones; scalloped edges. Muslin back; orange bias binding. Hand-quilted outline, crosshatch and floral motifs.

$600-$750

BROKEN STAR

C 1930

Maker unknown. Des Moines, Iowa.

Solid pink, yellow, green, red and white cotton sateen cloths and broadcloths; white cotton background; hand pieced. Sateen back; yellow binding. Hand-quilted outline on diamonds, wineglass on background. Probably a kit quilt.

$600-$750

BROKEN STAR

C 1930

Maker unknown. United States.

Red, yellows, pink, blues and cream cotton, solids on white, cotton background. Muslin back; white cotton binding. Hand quilted.

$600-$750

DOUBLE BROKEN STAR WITH FEATHERED EDGES

C 1930

Maker unknown. United States.

Gold, blue, yellow, green, red and blue cotton solids on white background; unique edging on two opposite sides; machine pieced. Cotton batting. White cotton back; white cotton binding on top and bottom, and straight edges on both sides, red cotton bias binding on the feathered pointed edges. Hand quilted.

$1,500-$2,500

SUNBURST

C 1870

Maker unknown. United States.

Black, acid yellow, double pink and white cotton solids and prints on acid yellow background; pink cotton border on one edge. Gray and tan paisley stripe cotton back (25" wide); back-to-front self-binding. Hand-quilted outline extending to diamond crosshatch.

$600-$750

SUNBURST VARIATION

C 1940

Maker unknown. United States.

Yellow and white cotton solids in sunbursts around circular centers; six borders: white/narrow yellow/narrow white/narrow yellow/white/wide yellow; hand pieced. White cotton back; white bias binding. Hand-quilted outline, crosshatch and clamshell.

$750-$1,000

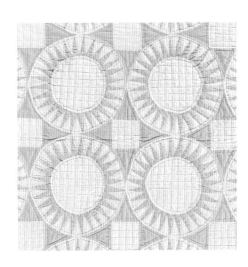

BLAZING STARS

C 1875

Maker unknown. United States.

Cotton prints, predominantly red, blue, brown, white and green on cream loose-weave cotton backgrounds; wide double pink cotton sashing; hand pieced. Muslin back; back-to-front self-binding. Hand quilted parallel lines.

$600-$750

BLAZING STARS

1937 (oral history).

Maker Lyde McCollum for the 12th birthday of Karen Bertelson of Minneapolis, Minn. Quilted by members of the Moravian Church of West Galena, Illinois. Various shades of yellow and orange cotton sateen on cream sateen background; unusual and intricate pieced border of orange and cream sateen. Hand quilted.

$600-$750

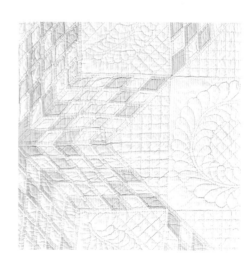

Signatures

Signature quilts have been made for at least 200 years. Some were made by the friends and families of the recipient, perhaps to commemorate a special occasion. Some traveled with a family moving to a new community, while others, especially from the 1860s on, were signed by members of a church or other group and then sold or auctioned to raise money for a worthy cause. They are known by several names: friendship quilts, album quilts or autograph quilts.

Because they were special to the recipients, they tended to be well cared for, and many survive, but sadly without documentation as to who made them or their purpose. Owners can now do research into the names on a quilt using the Internet, and interesting histories are emerging.

Dating can be simpler with signature quilts than with many other types, even if no dates are included on the quilt. The oldest quilts tend to have the names worked in cross-stitch, while after the development of non-damaging indelible inks in the 1830s, written signatures, dates, quotations and even pictures appear. Stem stitch and chain stitch embroidery occur on quilts dating from the 1870s on.

FRIENDSHIP ALBUM TOP

C 1900

Maker unknown. United States.

Multicolored cotton prints and solids with white crosses; yellow sashing; many blocks signed; blocks on point; yellow border.

$400–$600

FRIENDSHIP ALBUM

Dated 1849 in black cross-stitch
Maker possibly Chlor Woodward. Possibly New York.
Multicolored cotton solids and prints, predominantly reds, greens, and browns; white cotton sashing; all 56 blocks signed in ink by the same hand and set on point; hand pieced. Cotton batt. Muslin back; red dotted binding. Hand quilted cross hatch, channel, and parallel lines. Some staining.

$750-$1,000

COURTHOUSE SQUARE FRIENDSHIP TOP

20th century
Maker unknown. United States.
Multicolored cotton solids and prints; white cotton crosses and spacers; each block signed and set on point.

$250-$400

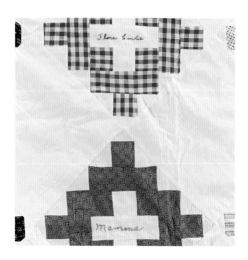

TURKEY TRACKS FRIENDSHIP QUILT

Dated 1842 and 1844

Maker unknown. Probably Minnesota.

Turkey red and white cotton blocks; white sashing; 72 names signed in ink, 15 locations listed; hand pieced. Cotton batting. Muslin back; cotton twill tape binding. Hand-quilted crosshatch, parallel lines and motifs, clamshell on sashing.

$2,000-$3,000

FRIENDSHIP ALBUM

Dated 1898

Maker Lydia Schuette of Dixon, Illinois., for the wife of her father, the Reverend Schuette.

Red cotton solids; white cotton background and sashing; signatures embroidered in red floss; narrow white cotton border. Muslin back; knife-edge binding. Hand-quilted cables.

$750-$1,000

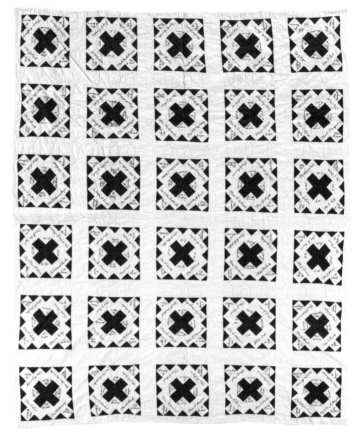

OHIO STAR FRIENDSHIP TOP

Dated 1915-1925

Maker unknown. Iowa.

Cotton shirtings, mainly grays and white; signatures and dates between 1915 and 1925; bright blue sashing and border.

$250-$400

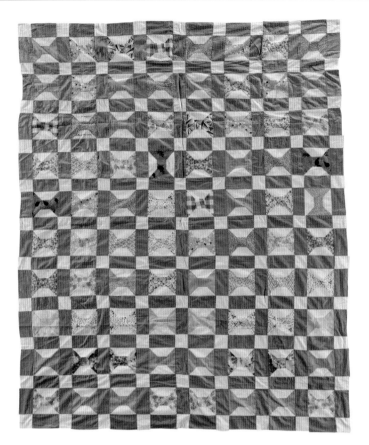

BOWTIE FRIENDSHIP QUILT

20th century

Maker unknown. United States.

Multicolored cotton solids and prints; purple cotton sashing with yellow cotton corners; bowties hand pieced, assembled by machine; some blocks are signed.

$250-$400

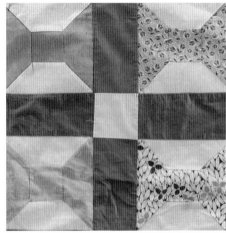

REDWORK SIGNATURE COVERLET

Dated 1892

Maker: members of the Elk Creek Valley Evangelical Lutheran Church, Osseo, Wisconsin.

Red floss embroidery on white cotton; elaborate scrolls held by birds carry the embroidered signatures; one scroll is inscribed "Komfermanter 1892." Blocks are assembled by machine with red, floss, feather stitching along the seams. White cotton back.

$750-$1,000

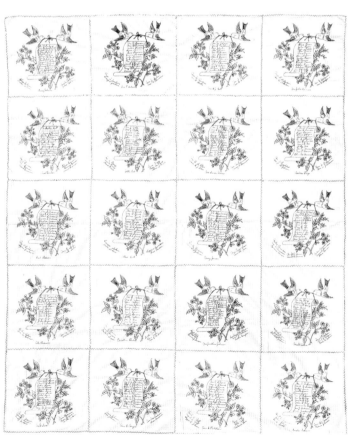

REDWORK SIGNATURE QUILT

1920s

Maker unknown. Marion, Ohio.

Red floss signatures embroidered on white cotton background; inscribed "Willing Workers." White cotton back. Hand-quilted crosshatch.

$600-$750

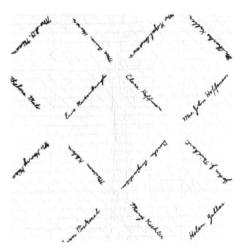

SIGNATURE BASKETS OF CHIPS

C 1900

Maker unknown. United States.

Multicolored cotton solids and prints, including indigos, double pinks, plaids, stripes and Turkey red for baskets; muslin backgrounds; faded red and white print zigzag sashing; last names, signed in ink, are mainly "Miner," "Meiner" and "Meany." Red and white cotton paisley print back; muslin binding.

$400-$600

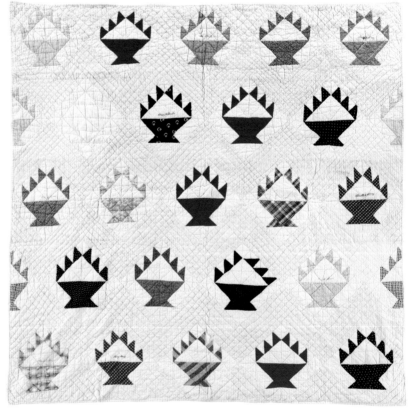

Curves

Curved shapes are trickier to sew than straight seams, so there are fewer examples of quilts with curved patterns, but the rarity and their sense of movement combine to make vintage curved-pattern quilts desirable. Patterns range from Drunkard's Path and its variations to Dresden Plate, Fan or Wagon Wheel, to Robbing Peter to Pay Paul, to Clamshell. Nineteenth-century examples are generally made in two colors, while multicolored versions are likely to be from the 20th century.

Double Wedding Ring is a curved pattern that was popular in the 1920s through the '40s. It was almost always made from prints, mainly scraps, except in the Amish communities, where it was generally fashioned from solids, often against a dark background of either blue or black.

ROBBING PETER TO PAY PAUL
C 1920
Maker unknown. United States.
Blue and white cotton; alternating blocks. Muslin back; blue binding. Wineglass and outline hand quilting.
$750-$1,000

ROBBING PETER TO PAY PAUL

C 1940

Maker unknown. United States, possibly Delaware. Double pink cotton and muslin, alternating blocks. Muslin back; back-to-front self-binding. Excellent quilting with marking still visible. Unwashed, probably unused.

$500-$750

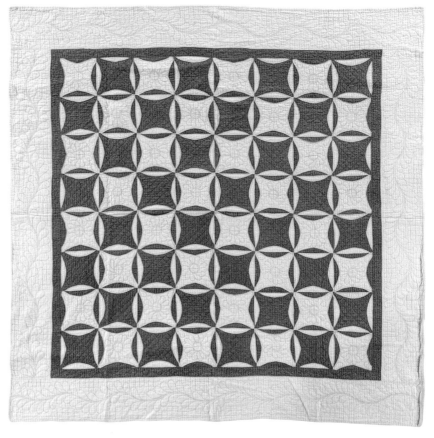

SNOWBALL

C 1885 (top)

Maker unknown, signed in pencil or ink: "Edwin from Grandma" in one corner. Quilted by Jo Peterson circa 2000. United States.

Blue and white cotton microprints, white cotton "snowballs;" white cotton border. Blue cotton print binding. Hand-quilted cable on border, floral motif in snowballs, outline on blocks.

$400-$600

CLAMSHELL
C 1890
Maker Jane Davis Simmons. Milwaukee, Wisconsin.
Hand-pieced cotton scraps, some faded and worn.
Blue and white check back, blue binding. Inferior
quilting.
$250-$400

HEARTS AND GIZZARDS
C 1940
Maker unknown. United States.
Pink and white cotton solids; pink cotton border. Pink
cotton back; back-to-front self-binding. Slight wear.
$250-$400

ROSE VARIATION COVERLET
C 1930
Maker unknown. United States.
Pink and white cotton pieced block. Hemmed but no batting or backing.
$100-$250

SCRAP DRUNKARD'S PATH
C 1930
Maker unknown. United States.
Cotton scraps, many fine-weave, and muslin. Cotton print back, also fine-weave; back-to-front self-binding. Tied.
$100-$250

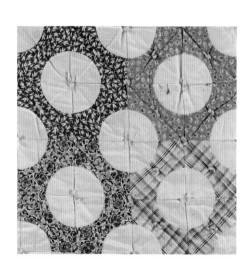

DRUNKARD'S PATH SET SQUARE

C 1890 (top)

Maker unknown. Quilted by Jo Peterson circa 2000.
United States.

Indigo print and white cotton traditional blocks set
square. New gray and blue back; new blue binding.
Hand quilted later.

$600-$750

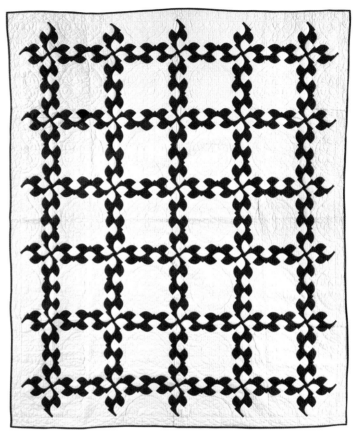

DRUNKARD'S PATH SET SQUARE WITH SPACERS

C 1920

Maker unknown. Iowa.

Blue cotton microdots and white cotton, traditional
blocks set square with blue cotton microdot spacers.
White, blue microdot, white cotton triple borders.
Muslin back, new white binding.

$750-$1,000

MULTICOLORED DRUNKARD'S PATH

C 1930

Maker unknown. United States.

Cotton scraps and muslin; four-patch cotton print circles applied in center of each spacer; scrappy scalloped ice cream cone border. Muslin back; blue binding. Hand-quilted sunflowers in each spacer.

$600-$750

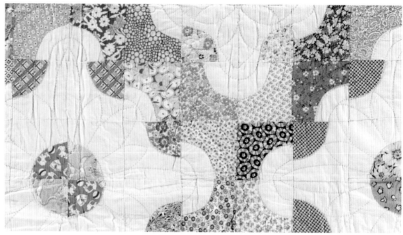

DRUNKARD'S PATH VARIATION
C 1950

Maker unknown. United States.

Blue and white cotton solids; traditional blocks with unusual set; blue border. White muslin back; white binding. Hand-quilted outline on blocks, wineglass in spacers, wave on border.

$600-$750

DRUNKARD'S PATH VARIATION
C 1870

Maker unknown. United States.

Blue and white microdot cotton print and muslin; traditional blocks set with muslin rectangles as spacers. Muslin back; back-to-front self-binding. Hand quilted crosshatch and wineglass.

$750-$1,000

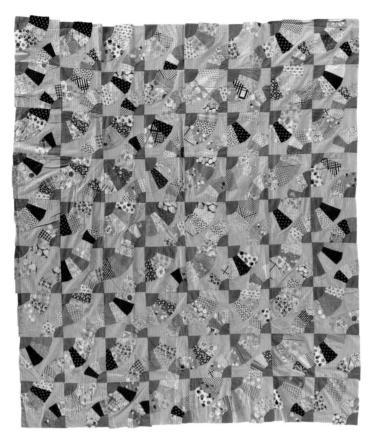

SNAKE IN THE HOLLOW TOP

C 1920
Maker unknown. United States, probably Iowa.
Multicolored cotton scraps with apricot cotton
"hollows;" machine pieced with hand appliquéd
corners.

$250-$400

NEW YORK BEAUTY

C 1930
Maker unknown. United States.
Blue and pink cotton solids on white backgrounds;
pink cotton inner border, blue cotton outer border.
White cotton back; pink cotton binding. Hand-quilted
outline and clamshell in blocks, pineapples in spaces,
cables in borders.

$1,500-$2,000

TURKEY TRACKS

C 1860

Maker unknown. United States.

Green, cream and cheddar cotton solids in blocks set on point; green cotton diagonal sashing; green cotton border, scalloped on the inner edge. Cream cotton back; cream cotton binding. Hand-quilted crosshatch in blocks, running feather in sashing and border. Pattern also known as Bible Tulip.

$1,000-$1,250

TURKEY TRACKS

C 1930

Maker unknown. United States.

Yellow and green cotton solids on white cotton background; green cotton border. Muslin back; knife-edge binding. Hand-quilted floral motifs in spaces, cables in border. Pattern was once called Wandering Foot.

$750-$1,000

WHIG'S DEFEAT

C 1920

Maker unknown, a member of the Powell family of
Pensacola, Fla., formerly from Roaring River, Tenn.,
direct descendants of Roger Williams of Rhode Island.
United States.

Red and green cotton solids on white backgrounds;
white cotton spacers and border; hand pieced. White
cotton back; green cotton binding. Hand-quilted
outline in blocks, feathers in spacers.

$750-$1,000

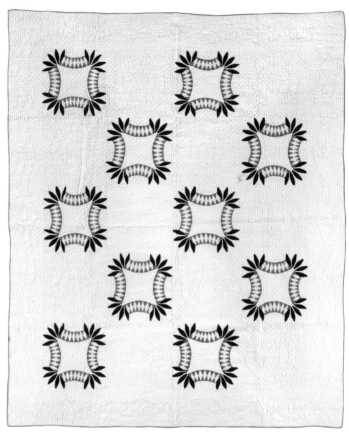

DRESDEN PLATE MINIATURES

C 1940

Maker unknown. United States.

Multicolored cotton scraps appliquéd to white cotton
background blocks; round-edge plates measure six
inches in diameter; bright blue cotton sashing with
red cotton corners; wide white border. Muslin back;
blue binding applied knife-edge. Hand-quilted grids
in the centers of the plates, loops in the corners;
unusual five-petaled flower and vine motif on border.

$750-$1,000

DRESDEN PLATES

C 1930

Maker unknown. United States.

Multicolored cotton solids and prints; large yellow centers; round-edge plates appliquéd to white cotton background; multicolored prints alternate with solid yellow cotton on the pieced ice cream cone border. Cotton batting. White cotton back; knife-edge binding with a yellow cotton facing on the back. Hand-quilted feather wreaths in centers and where blocks meet; plus flowers, hanging diamonds, parallel lines and ditch.

$400-$600

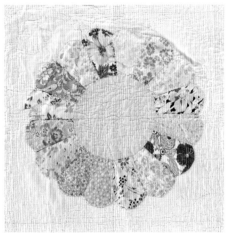

DRESDEN PLATE

C 1935

Maker unknown. United States.

Multicolored cotton prints and solids for pointed-edge plates with yellow cotton centers appliquéd to salmon background squares. Salmon back; knife-edge binding. Hand quilted in the ditch.

$250-$400

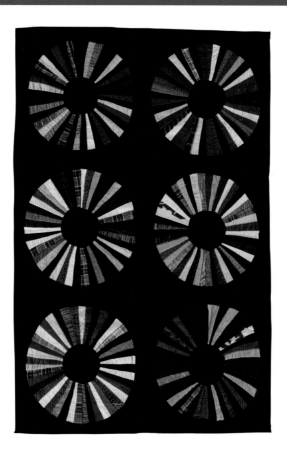

WAGON WHEELS THROW

C 1935

Maker unknown. United States.

Multicolored wools, velvets, silks, linens, cottons, flannels, sateens and voiles in solids, prints, plaids and stripes; hand-sewn fan variation pattern on muslin foundations; assembled by machine. No back; black binding. Machine-quilted outlines.

$400-$600

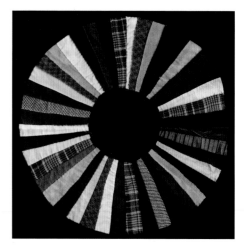

DOUBLE WEDDING RING

C 1920

Maker unknown; made for the owner's grandmother's wedding. Midwestern United States. Multicolored cotton scraps; pink connectors; muslin centers and melons; outer rings form scalloped border. Muslin back; pink cotton binding. Hand-quilted floral motif in centers; possibly an Eastern Star symbol in the melons. Some staining on the back.

$250-$400

DOUBLE WEDDING RING

C 1930

Maker unknown. United States.

Pastel multicolored cotton scraps; muslin centers and melons; squared edges. Muslin back; blue binding. Machine quilted zigzag.

$100-$250

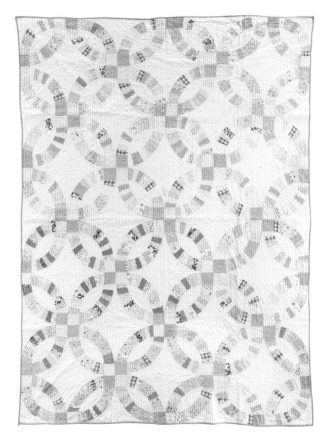

DOUBLE WEDDING RING

C 1920

Maker unknown. United States.

Multicolored cotton scraps; blue and white print and cream four-patch connectors; white centers and melons; outer rings form scalloped border. Muslin back; pink bias binding. Hand-quilted outline and motifs in centers. Minor staining.

$250-$400

CHAPTER 3

APPLIQUÉ

Appliqué is the name given to the ancient decorative technique of applying a cutout shape of one fabric to a background of a different material. It has been used to adorn clothing and household textiles in virtually every civilization throughout the world for millennia, but it reached an apex with appliqué quilts of the 19th century.

One of the earliest forms of appliqué on bedcovers was the use of motifs cut from highly desirable and expensive chintz from India, which were then sewn to a less costly plain background fabric, a technique known as broderie perse, or Persian embroidery. Examples can be found as the central medallions on British frame quilts from the late 1800s and early 1900s. Such quilts are rare and most examples are safely housed in museum collections.

By the middle of the 1800s appliqué was becoming popular, and most of the vintage appliqué quilts in private hands were made in the century between 1850 and 1950. Styles changed dramatically over that time, but one factor remained steady—by far, the most numerous motifs are floral.

Appliqué quilts were normally hand stitched, but after a practical sewing machine was patented in 1846, quiltmakers began to use this new technology not just for piecing and quilting, but also for appliqué. Collectors differ in their attitude to vintage machine appliqué, but well-done machine topstitching should not take value from an example that can be authentically dated to the mid-19th century.

Many desirable appliqué quilts were made between about 1870 and 1900, when the fashion was for bright colors, especially red, green, double pink, yellow and cheddar orange on a cream or white background. Most were made in blocks and many have elaborate appliquéd borders. At the same time, many charming folk art quilts were produced, usually in the same color palette, but with less sophisticated designs and less accomplished stitching.

The 20th-century heyday of appliqué took place during the 1920s and '30s, when the Colonial Revival sparked a renewed interest in quiltmaking in general. Patterns and kits were designed and sold in huge quantities, and again the motifs were mainly floral, with the notable exception of Sunbonnet Sue and her myriad spin-offs. Kit quilts were not particularly valued until recently, but their comparative rarity and simple yet pleasing designs have made well-executed examples very collectible.

In this chapter
162 Sunbonnet Sue
164 Pictorals and Florals

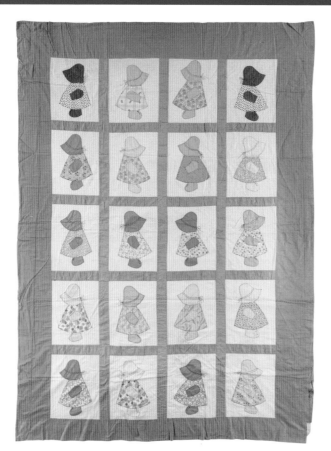

SUNBONNET SUE

C 1925

Maker unknown. Midwestern United States. Multicolor prints and solids hand appliquéd on white cotton background; black running stitch and embroidered details; pink cotton sashing and border. Striped flannel batting. Large-scale print back; straight binding. Minimal hand quilting in the ditch.

$400-$600

SHEPHERDESS SUE

C 1925

Maker unknown. Midwestern United States. Multicolored cotton prints and solids hand appliquéd on cream cotton background; black embroidered details including shepherdess's staffs; blue cotton sashing. Cream cotton back; blue binding. Unused and never washed.

$400-$600

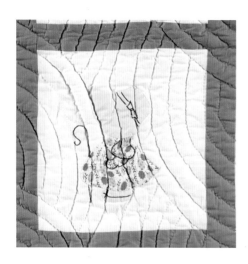

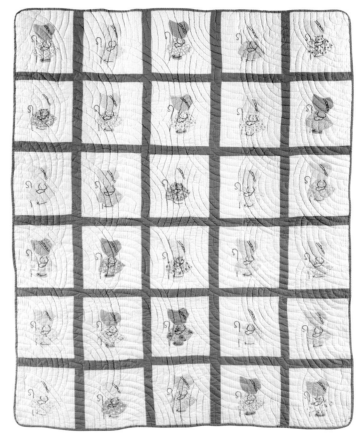

SUNBONNET SUE ON POINT TOP

C 1925
Maker unknown. Washington.
Multicolored cotton prints and solids hand appliquéd on cream background; black outline stitch worked with floss; four blocks on point in the center, surrounded by yellow frame, then 20 more appliqué blocks on point with large yellow setting triangles in each corner; assembled by machine.
$100 or less

SUNBONNET SUE

Dated 1935
Maker unknown. Midwestern United States.
Multicolored cotton prints and solids hand appliquéd on muslin background; details embroidered in black floss; purple sashing with green corners; green border. Muslin back; purple binding.
$600–$750

COLONIAL LADIES

C 1935

Maker unknown. Canada.

Multicolored cotton prints and solids hand appliquéd on white background; embroidered details; yellow and white triple sashing with white corners; double borders of yellow and white cotton. White cotton back; prairie point binding alternating yellow and white points. Hand quilted with crosshatch and cables.

$400-$600

BUTTERFLIES

1920s

Maker unknown. United States, probably Midwestern. Cotton prints hand appliquéd on white background with buttonhole stitch; purple sashing and border with pink corners. Pink binding.

$100-$250

HICKORY LEAF

C 1890

Maker Elizabeth Jung Endlich (1861-1951). Wayne, Wisconsin.

Red motifs hand appliquéd to white background; red and white pieced-diamond sashing; red and white triple border on two sides; plain red border at top and bottom. Tweed blanket batting. Red binding. Made for the wedding of Mrs. Endlich's daughter Alvina Endlich Schmidt.

$600-$750

OAK LEAF AND REEL

Dated 1844

Maker unknown. Signed "ES". Minnesota.

Dotted blue and white cotton hand appliquéd to white background; small blue star flowers throughout; blue hand appliquéd oak trees along edges. White back; front to back self-binding. Outline hand quilting.

$2,000-$3,000

OAK LEAF AND REEL

C 1875

Maker unknown. Probably United States, possibly Britain.

Cadet blue cotton hand appliquéd on muslin background; wide border with trees and dovecotes; lovebirds and hearts could signify a wedding quilt. Cotton batting. Muslin back; back-to-front self-binding. Minimal quilting.

$400-$600

OAK LEAF AND REEL

C 1875

Maker unknown. United States.

Red, green and yellow cotton solids hand appliquéd to muslin background; inner and outer borders pieced red and white triangles. Muslin back; back-to-front self-binding. Some fading.

$400-$600

LANCASTER ROSE FOUR-BLOCK

Dated 1915 (on back binding)

Maker unknown. United States, probably Midwest. Solid pink, rose, faded green and orange cottons hand appliquéd to white background; pink, rose and green cotton triple borders. Cotton batting. White cotton back; back-to-front self-binding. Hand quilted crosshatch, spaced one inch apart.

$750-$1,000

FOUR-BLOCK ROSE

C 1875

Maker unknown. United States.

Red and green cottons hand appliquéd on white background; hand-appliquéd border vine is very faded. Muslin back; very frayed binding. Considerable wear overall.

$600-$750

FOUR-BLOCK FLORAL SPRAY KIT QUILT

1930s

Maker unknown. United States.

Pastel cotton solids on white whole-cloth background; some shaded embroidery; pink border scalloped on the inner edge. Hand quilting follows the pattern.

$600-$750

FOUR-BLOCK CHARIOT WHEEL

C 1870

Maker unknown. United States.

Red, yellow and green faded to blue-gray cottons hand appliquéd to white background; red/yellow/red/white border. Muslin back; brown binding; may be later than the top. Hand quilted close crosshatch and outline on the blocks, parallel lines on the border.

$2,000-$3,000

CAPE COD BASKETS

1930

Maker unknown. United States.

Pastel cotton solids hand appliquéd to white cotton whole-cloth background; baskets brown bias strips arranged medallion style with central floral wreath and floral border with shallow scallops. Pattern from the Needlecraft Co., cost $2.98 + 27 cents postage and packing. White back; yellow bias binding. Elaborate quilting.

$1,000-$1,500

CAPE COD BASKETS COVERLET

1930

Maker unknown. United States.

See previous quilt for particulars of design and fabrics, but this is a non-quilted coverlet with no batting.

$400-$600

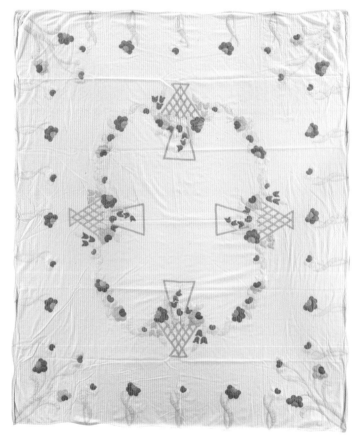

CAESAR'S CROWN

1870s

Maker unknown. United States or Britain.

Red, yellow and green cotton prints hand appliquéd on white English linen background; red and green swag border. White cotton back; white binding. Elaborate quilting. Never washed.

$2,000-$3,000

SCHERENSCHNITTE

C 1860

Maker unknown. United States.

Blue cotton microdot paper-cut motifs hand appliquéd on white background; blue cotton floral vine border appliqué on three sides. White cotton back; back-to-front self-binding. Hand-quilted outline and parallel lines in blocks, clamshell in border.

$3,000-$5,000

PALM TREE

Dated 1852

Maker Helen E. Lowry: signed. United States.
Red/yellow cotton print hand appliquéd to white
cotton background: 20 main motifs, connectors, and
border motifs; red and white saw-tooth edge. White
cotton back; front-to-back binding. Elaborate quilting.
$3,000-$5,000

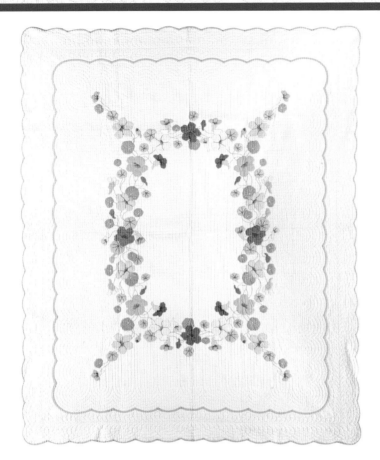

NASTURTIUM MEDALLION GARLAND

1930s
Maker unknown. United States.
Yellow, orange, gold, peach and green cotton solids hand appliquéd to white cotton whole-cloth background; shaded embroidery; peach scalloped inner border, wide white outer border. White back; peach scalloped binding. Hand quilted: echo in the center, running feather in the border. Kit.

$750-$1,000

ROSE MEDALLION

1916-1920
Maker probably Mrs. Nicholas Lehr. St. Paul, Minnesota.
Pastel floral cottons hand appliquéd on white cotton whole-cloth background; central motif encircled by floral garland; single flowers in each corner. White cotton back; green bias scalloped binding. Hand-quilted following kit pattern.

$600-$750

TREE OF LIFE MEDALLION

1950s

Maker unknown. United States.

Cotton prints and solids hand appliquéd on white cotton whole-cloth background; embroidered embellishments; Jacobean-style floral motifs in center and corners. White cotton back; green bias scalloped binding. Elaborate quilting. Kit.

$600-$750

EAGLE MEDALLION

C 1935

Maker unknown. United States.

Blue cotton eagle, stars, urns and floral motifs hand appliquéd on white cotton whole-cloth background; blue swag border. Muslin back; knife-edge binding. Hand-quilted crosshatch. Kit or pattern.

$600-$750

WHIG ROSE

C 1850

Maker unknown. United States.

Red, green and cheddar cotton prints and solids hand appliquéd on white cotton background; red inner and green outer borders; blocks set on point with white cotton sashing. Red-microprint binding. Hand quilted: crosshatch on blocks, running feather on sashing, cable on green border.

$1,500-$2,000

ROSE WREATH TOP

C 1920

Green, pink and orange cotton solids hand appliquéd on white cotton background; hand pieced.

$100-$250

WHIG ROSE

C 1860

Maker unknown. United States, probably Midwest. Cheddar, red and fugitive-green cotton solids hand appliquéd on white background; nine blocks set edge to edge. Muslin back; red binding. Minimal quilting.

$1,500-$2,000

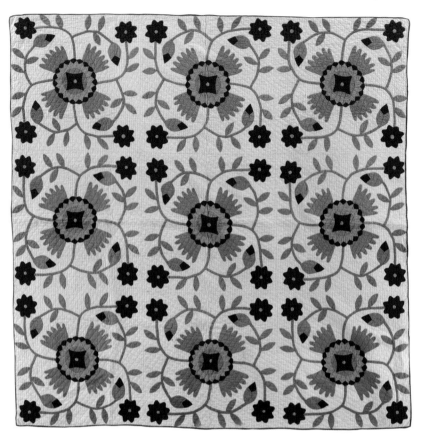

ROSEBUDS AND RIBBONS

1850s

Maker unknown. United States, possibly Ohio. Double pink and green cotton prints hand appliquéd on white background; wide leaf and flower hand appliquéd border. Muslin back; muslin binding with double pink piping insert. Elaborate close hand quilting.

$2,000-$3,000

JONQUILS

1930s

Maker unknown. United States.

Yellow, gold and green cotton solids hand appliquéd on white cotton background; narrow triple inner border of yellow, white and green; wider white outer border. White cotton back; green binding. Hand-quilted parallel lines. Stearns and Foster pattern from Mountain Mist batting packaging.

$750-$1,000

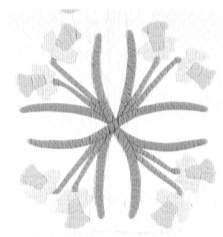

NEW YORK FLORAL

1860

Maker unknown. Probably New York.

Red and green (fading to blue) cotton solids hand appliquéd on white background; nine blocks with cherry vines between main motifs and on border; cherries are stuffed. Muslin back; green (blue) binding piped with red. Hand-quilted clamshell and outline.

$1,500-$2,000

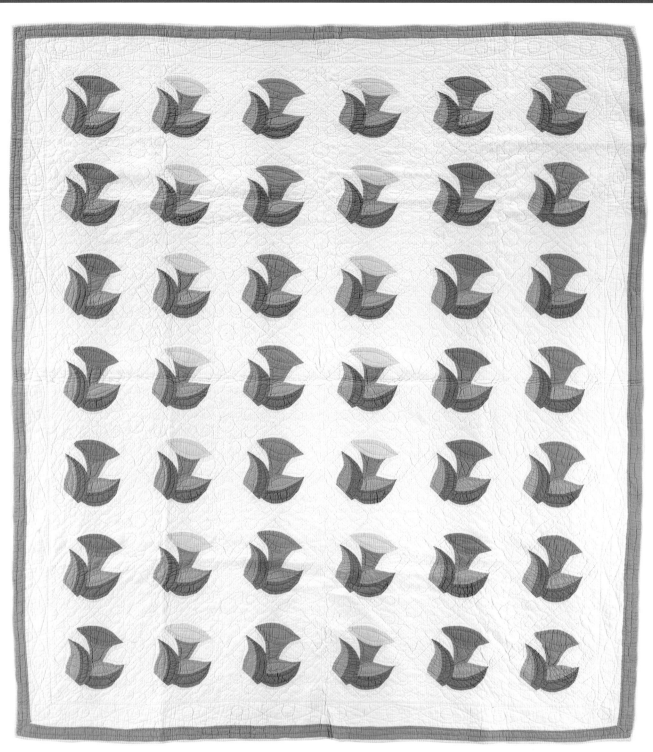

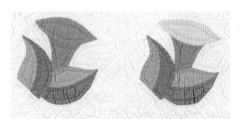

ART DECO TULIPS

1930s

Maker unknown. Mid-Atlantic United States.

Pink, yellow, orange, purple and green cotton solids hand appliquéd on white background; white and orange borders. White cotton back; back-to-front self-binding. Probably a kit.

$400-$600

TULIP COVERLET

C 1960

Maker unknown. Southern United States.
Yellow, orange and green cotton solids hand
appliquéd on white background; pale yellow framing
border with gold corners; white scalloped outer
border. No batting. Muslin back; gold bias binding.
Simple well-executed hand quilting. Kit or pattern.
Some staining.

$250-$400

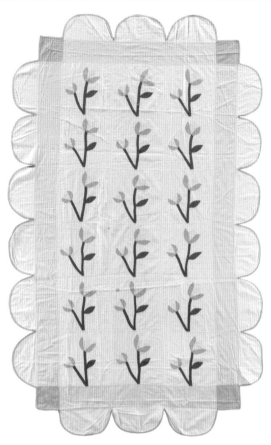

TULIP MEDALLION

C 1935

Maker unknown. United States.
Yellow, gold and green cotton solids hand appliquéd
on white background; central square motif and
corner motifs; wide yellow border. Muslin back;
yellow binding. Hand-quilted diamond grid. Stearns
and Foster pattern from Mountain Mist batting
packaging. Slight staining.

$400-$600

TULIP GARDEN

C 1955

Maker unknown. United States.

Red, green, yellow, pink, purple, blue, orange, brown and turquoise cotton solids hand appliquéd on white whole-cloth background; yellow inner and white outer borders. Cotton batting. White cotton back; white binding. Hand quilting. Probably a kit or pattern.

$600-$750

FLOWER BLOCKS

C 1945

Maker unknown. United States.

Multicolored cotton scraps hand appliquéd on white cotton background; each flower has eight petals, a yellow center and a green stem; peach sashing with green corners; scalloped peach border on two opposite sides. Muslin back; peach binding.

$400-$600

LAUREL LEAVES

C 1860

Maker unknown. United States.

Green and red cotton prints hand appliquéd on white background; red horizontal and white vertical sashing between blocks; white inner and green outer borders. White back; red binding. Heavy hand quilting.

$750-$1,000

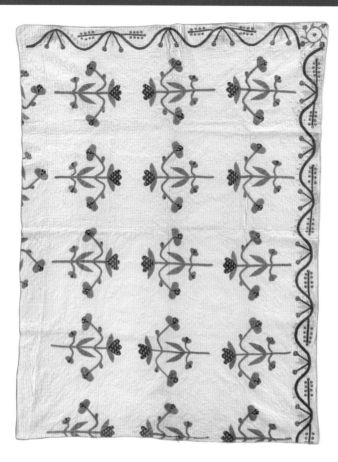

PEONY

C 1880

Maker unknown, "L" embroidered on the back. Kentucky.

Red and green cottons hand appliquéd to white background; appliquéd border on two adjacent sides worked in completely different fabrics. Muslin back; faded red binding. Some staining. Possibly cut down from a larger quilt.

$250-$400

MORNING GLORIES

1950s

Maker unknown. United States.

Blue and apricot cotton solids hand appliquéd to white cotton background; embroidered details; blue sashing; apricot border. Muslin back; blue binding. Fine hand quilting. Pattern or kit.

$250-$400

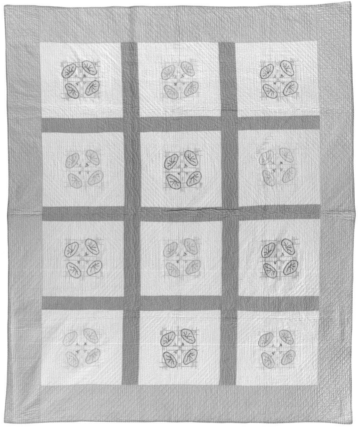

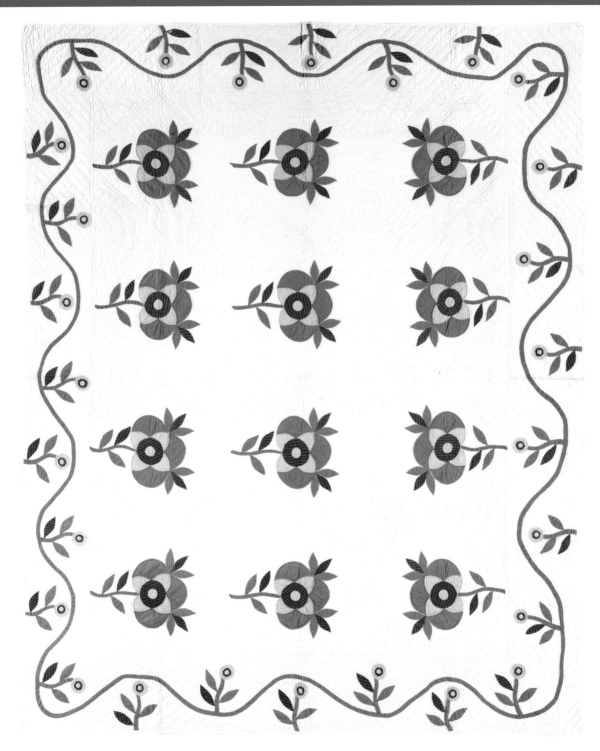

POMEGRANATE

C 1860

Maker unknown. United States.

Red, pink and green cotton prints hand appliquéd on white cotton whole-cloth background;
vine border is green cotton print with flowers made from yo-yos in light and dark red and
yellow; blocks are set on point with white spacers. White cotton back; white binding. Hand
quilted outlines on motifs, feather wreaths in spacers, and parallel lines in border.

$750-$1,000

CHAPTER 4

EMBELLISHED QUILTS

Embroidered Quilts

Embroidered quilts became fashionable in the last quarter of the 19th century, and the fad lasted until the late 1920s. Cross-stitched quilts enjoyed a heyday in the early 20th century, but were outnumbered by the wildly popular redwork quilts, which, with their later cousins the bluework, or blackwork, or some other color, were widely made beginning in the 1880s.

Sold by the thousands were patterns stamped on muslin squares in a variety of motifs, ranging from natural forms, like flowers to animals to patriotic images and slogans, to depictions of nursery rhymes and alphabets. Most were outlined in stem stitch using red cotton embroidery floss, which by then was dyed with colorfast Turkey red dye.

A large number of embroidered examples are actually coverlets without batting or quilting. Quite a few redwork quilts are dated, and the motifs themselves can help determine when a quilt was made. Early images mirrored those found on many crazy quilts (see pages 191-197), and once the craze took hold, quiltmakers used simple line drawings from popular children's books or patterns published in magazines.

Stamped blocks known as "penny squares" became widely available after the 1901 Pan-American Exposition in Buffalo, N.Y., and form the basis for many embroidered quilts. By the 1920s themed blocks and patterns were available both for outline work and cross-stitch. Many examples were kits that included the stamped fabric and thread. Cross-stitch was also used on some simple quilts to hold the layers together, acting as the quilting.

The quality of the embroidery, the charm or sophistication of the design, and the overall condition of the quilt are the important factors in collecting.

In this chapter
185 Embroidered Quilts
191 Crazy Quilts

REDWORK QUILT

Dated 1893

Maker unknown. New England.

Penny squares on white muslin, mainly flowers and birds, some repeated; four fan blocks, each set differently. Substantial wear on one block. Muslin back; wide poorly executed binding, possibly later.

$250-$400

REDWORK & EMBROIDERED QUILT

C 1930

Maker Ira Hosto Zoelzer, age 12-14, grandmother of the owner. Wisconsin.

Embroidered penny squares with typical flowers, bird, etc., and many words; dated "April 11 1915," thought by owner to be the maker's birthday; yellow setting squares and border. Knife-edge binding.

$400-$600

REDWORK COVERLET

1920s

Makers unidentified, owner's mother Elizabeth Alice Twing Bruning (b. 19925) remembers watching the maid in her home working on it when she was a child. Holyoke, Massachusetts. Embroidered penny squares of white muslin, set side by side; herringbone stitch along each seam and outside edges. Knife-edge binding.

$250-$400

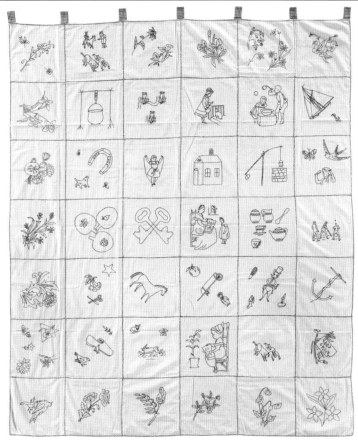

CROSS-STITCHED WEDDING QUILT

1890

Maker unknown, made for the wedding of the owner's great-grandmother, Louisa Marie Steinmetz (Mrs. John Francis) Ewalt (1863-1955). Midwestern United States. Stamped cream cotton blocks cross-stitched with gold floss; cheddar cotton spacers, pale yellow border. Yellow cotton back; cheddar binding.

$600-$750

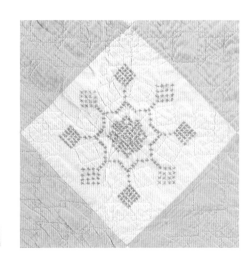

FLORAL EMBROIDERED AND APPLIQUED COVERLET

C 1930

Maker unknown. United States.

Yellow flowers applied to white cotton ground, embroidered leaves; yellow scalloped border; two cut-out corners. Cotton back; knife-edge binding.

$250-$400

EMBROIDERED STATE BIRDS

Dated 1947

Maker Lillian Heidtke. Milwaukee, Wisconsin.

Beautifully executed embroidered pattern blocks of 48 state birds, white cotton, multicolored floss; pink sashing and borders; machine pieced. Pink back, front to back self-binding. Minimal hand quilting.

$600-$750

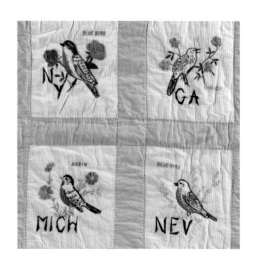

BALTIMORE ALBUM-STYLE CROSS-STITCH KIT QUILT

C 1970

Maker unknown. United States, possibly Midwest. Cross-stitch on white cotton ground, bright floss in typical Baltimore colors; pink and red sawtooth embroidered border; machine pieced. White cotton back; back to front self-binding. Hand quilted, overall grid.

$600-$750

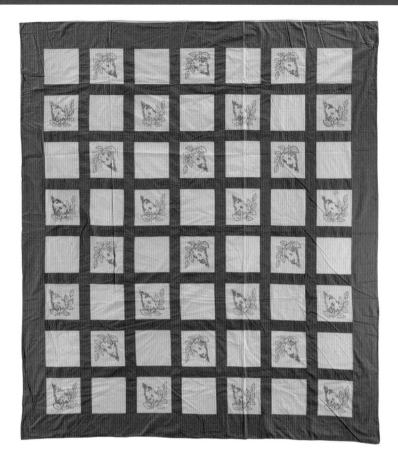

FLORAL EMBROIDERED COVERLET
20th century
Maker unknown. United States.
Floral cream cotton pattern, purple and green; floss; alternating cream setting blocks; purple sashing and border.
$100-$250

DOUBLE IRISH CHAIN WITH CROSS-STITCH QUILTING

C 1900 (top). Back, binding, and quilting 1970s. Maker Ira Hosto Zoelzer, age 12-14, grandmother of the owner. Wisconsin.

Embroidered penny squares with typical flowers, bird, etc., and many words; dated "April 11 1915," thought by owner to be the maker's birthday; yellow setting squares and border. Knife-edge binding.

$400-$600

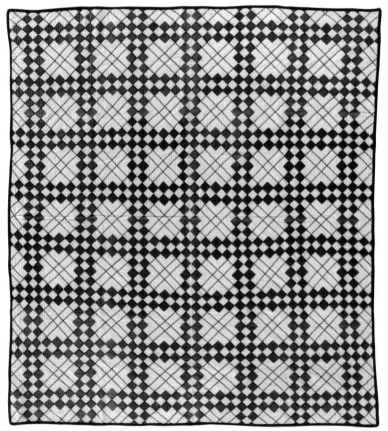

Crazy Quilts

Crazy quilts generally end up in a category of their own, because they combine piecing, appliqué and embroidery. When quiltmaking reached its zenith in the last quarter of the 19th century, crazy quilts became one of the most popular, and certainly the most recognizable, types. The most stunning examples are usually made from dressmaking scraps of fine fabrics, such as silk, taffeta, velvet and satin, and are embellished with embroidery worked most often in silk or cotton floss.

Victorian ladies on both sides of the Atlantic created crazy quilts in large quantities, and because many of them are signed and dated, they are valuable documents both for collectors and historians. American crazies are often worked on a foundation of muslin or old shirting in squares or rectangles that are pieced together into "contained" crazy quilts, while British examples are usually pieced on a single piece of backing fabric, with the stitching begun in one corner.

Interesting artifacts appear in crazy quilts, from ribbons and tassels to cigarette silks, ribbon-work flowers and metal charms. The surface decoration tends to be heavy and elaborate, with each patch of fabric outlined in feather stitch, herringbone or chain stitch, and many areas are embroidered with motifs ranging from owls and flowers to horseshoes and pet animals.

One recurring image is a fan, usually pieced, that turns up on most crazy quilts. These quilts tend to be fragile and were not intended to be used as bedcovers but as parlor throws. The fabrics in many examples have shattered, and they need to be looked after carefully.

Not all crazy quilts were made of fine fabrics, however. Utilitarian versions were also widely made from wool, but also occasionally from cotton, especially in the United States, and were intended for the bedroom. They were usually made in the "contained crazy" format, and while each patch is generally outlined with decorative stitching, as on the parlor examples, the embroidery is worked in cotton floss or wool yarn, and embroidered motifs seldom appear. The colors are somber, typical of wool fabrics, but red, pink, blue and green do appear, as well.

CONTAINED CRAZY QUILT
C 1880
Maker unknown. United States.
Mainly velvets crazy-pieced on 30 foundation blocks; good decorative stitching. Beige silk back; black silk binding.
$1,500-$2,000

DOUBLE-SIDED CRAZY QUILT
C 1890
Maker: a member of the family of Caroline Quinn Fleager. Probably Texas or Tennessee.
Wools and a few cottons crazy-pieced on 16 foundation blocks; decorative stitching worked with wool yarn. Pieced back of wool scraps joined in strippy form. Plaid binding. Closely tied with yarn. Some damage (moths?).
$250-$400

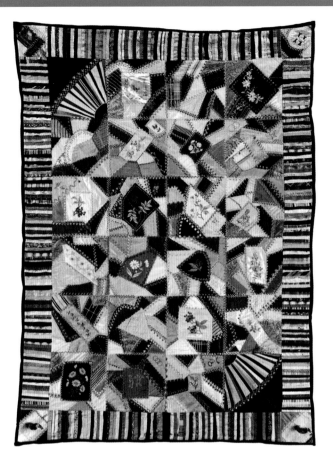

SILK CRAZY QUILT

C 1890

Maker unknown. Probably central New York. Dressmaking silks, taffetas, brocades and velvets crazy-pieced on 22 foundation blocks; strip-pieced fans on two opposite corner blocks; excellent decorative stitching worked with silk floss; border pieced from thin strips of similar fabrics; crazy-pieced corner blocks. Black silk binding.

$1,500-$2,000

CONTAINED CRAZY QUILT

C 1900

Maker Harriet Dunn. Sardinia, Ohio. Wools, silks and cottons crazy-pieced on nine foundation blocks; excellent decorative stitching worked in cotton and silk floss; wide burgundy wool border. Gray cotton stripe back; burgundy wool binding. Some wear on border.

$250-$400

CRAZY-PIECED THROW
Dated 1893
Maker unknown: signed "MTL." United States.
Crazy-pieced dressmaking scraps; bright-colored silk flowers scattered over the surface; excellent decorative stitching; brown velvet border. Brown cotton back; knife-edge binding. Some shattered silks.
$1,500-$2,000

CONTAINED CRAZY QUILT
C 1910
Maker unknown. Midwestern United States. Wool scraps crazy-pieced on foundation blocks; one motif resembles a church and steeple, and when turned upside down, it becomes a child's dress; excellent decorative embroidery. Plaid striped flannel back; brown binding. Closely tied.
$750-$1,000

CONTAINED CRAZY QUILT

C 1885

Maker unknown. Three Bridges, New Jersey.

Assorted dressmaking scraps crazy-pieced on foundation blocks and strips; one corner fan; dated partly by a Stevengraph ribbon of a foxhunting scene, excellent decorative stitching with a brown velvet border. Pre-quilted satin comforter back; knife-edge binding.

$2,000-$3,000

CRAZY QUILT THROW

C 1890

Maker unknown. Probably Wisconsin.

Dressmaking scraps, mainly silks and velvets, crazy-pieced on nine foundation blocks and embellished with ribbon-work flowers; excellent decorative stitching. Cotton back. Black polyester binding added later.

$1,000-$1,500

COTTON CRAZY QUILT

C 1900

Maker unknown. United States, probably New England.

Traditional Monkey Wrench blocks bordered with crazy strips and crazy blocks worked on a foundation. Black-and-white cotton mourning print back, back-to-front self-binding. Tied with wool yarn and white store string.

$250-$400

UTILITARIAN CRAZY QUILT

C 1910

Maker unknown. United States, probably Midwestern.

Mainly wool scraps crazy-pieced on foundation blocks; decorative feather stitching. Pieced plaid back; back-to-front self-binding. Double cross-hatch quilting. Some wear.

$100-$250

WOOL CONTAINED CRAZY QUILT

Dated 1920

Maker unknown. United States, probably Midwestern.

Wool scraps crazy-pieced on 16 foundation blocks; nice decorative stitching. Wool batting. Striped wool back; back-to-front self-binding. Tied with thin yarn.

$250-$400

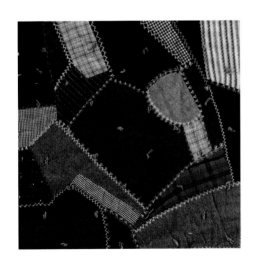

Crib Quilts

Vintage crib quilts, baby quilts or cradle quilts are small treasures that have withstood the ravages of time, and the numerous washings, to which most will have been subjected. They are highly desirable collectibles, partly because they are small and easier to store than full-size quilts, but also because their individuality sets them apart. They are also rare; as objects beloved by their recipients, they were heavily used, and many did not survive, while those that did often show signs of how much "loving" they received.

Because they are popular items with collectors, it is important to make sure that prices reflect the quality and veracity of the piece. Watch out for so-called crib quilts that are actually pieces cut from larger quilts and re-bound (see Fakes, page 10-11). While these may be vintage in themselves, the prices may be inflated over the value of larger quilts. It's possible that, say, four large-scale blocks made up a quilt that was only ever used for a baby, but the blocks in most true crib quilts are smaller in scale than their bed-size counterparts, and will have a matching or coordinated border rather than just a bound edge.

Among the most collectible types of crib quilts are those with small-scale blocks and kit or pattern quilts from the first half of the 20th century. Because many, if not most, crib quilts were made as gifts for a specific baby, they often come with some documentation or provenance, which enhances their value.

In this chapter
199 Crib Quilts
221 Doll Quilts

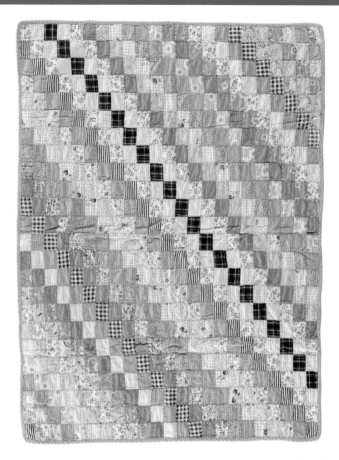

ONE-PATCH SQUARES: DIAGONAL ROWS
C 1940
Maker unknown. United States.
Bright cotton solids and prints set in diagonal rows.
Blue binding.
$100-$250

BOSTON COMMONS TOP
C 1950
Maker unknown. United States.
Cotton prints and solids, mainly blue and orange;
squares set on point. Some squares missing along
one outer row. Hand pieced.
$100 or less

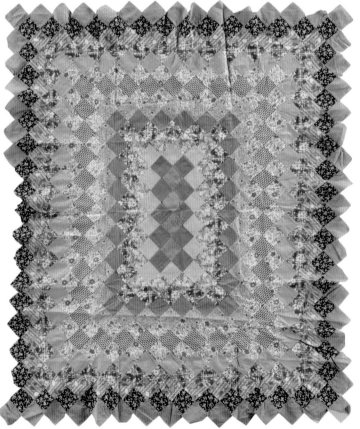

ECONOMY BLOCK STRIPPY CRIB QUILT

C 1855

Maker unknown. Probably New England.

Cotton prints, plaids and stripes; background small-scale floral stripe; hand pieced. Cotton batting. Blue and white striped binding. Hand quilted in clamshell. Some restoration on red fabrics.

$400-$600

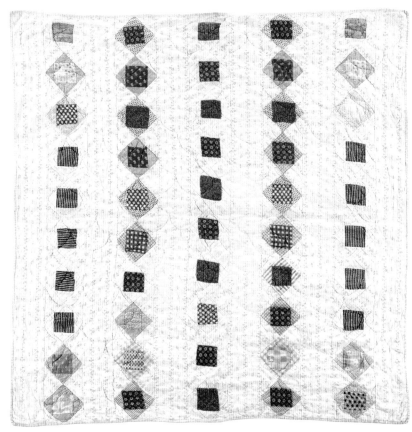

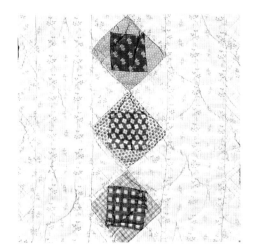

TWO-BLOCK CRIB QUILT

C 1900

Maker unknown. Britain.

Cotton prints, solids and stripes; alternating Hourglass and Rail Fence blocks. Red and white striped back. Muslin binding. Tied with pink cotton yarn.

$100-$250

Chapter 5: Small Quilts **201**

FOUR-PATCH COVERLET

Dated 1955

Maker "Grandma Galbreth," babysitter of owner.
Anderson Indiana.

Cotton prints and solids, scraps, some fading.
Muslin back; blue binding. Hand quilted with long
running stitch.

$100-$250

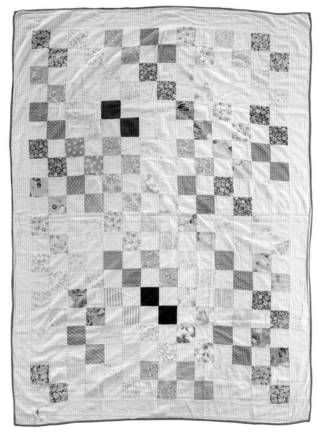

FOUR-PATCH CRIB QUILT

1930-1940

Maker unknown. Made for Jane Lincoln, Minneapolis,
Minnesota.

Cotton prints and solids with setting squares, mainly
yellow but some green; faded gray border. Yellow
back. Diagonal quilting.

$100-$250

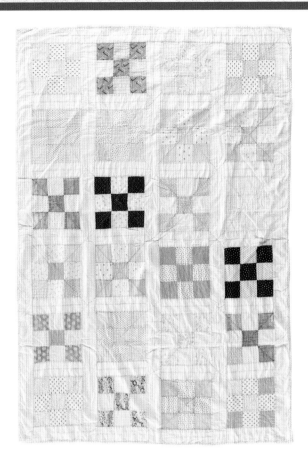

NINE-PATCH CRIB QUILT

20th century
Maker unknown. United States.
Cotton prints and shirtings, some double pinks;
faded; pink and white striped sashing and border.
Muslin back, pink and white stripe bias cut binding.
Machine quilted.
$100-$250

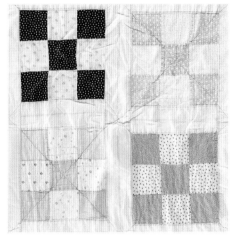

NINE-PATCH CRIB QUILT TOP

C 1900
Maker unknown. United States.
Alternating cotton solids and stripes set adjacent;
triple border: various pieced purple stripes, solid blue,
pieced black and white stripes.
$100-$250

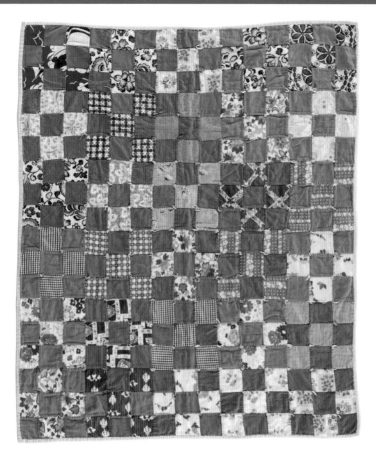

NINE-PATCH CRIB QUILT

C 1950

Maker unknown. United States.

Solid blue cottons alternating with prints, stripes and checks; hand pieced. Muslin back; back-to-front self-binding. Tied, pink floss in central section, blue at top and bottom.

$100-$250

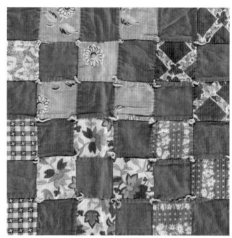

LIGHT AND DARK LOG CABIN

C 1920

Maker unknown. United States.

Cotton prints, yellow centers; logs ¼" wide. Blanket batting? New back and binding, machine stitched. Tied with white string.

$250-$400

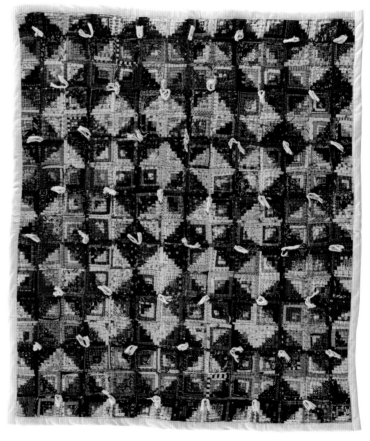

MULTICOLOR PINWHEELS

1890s fabrics.

Maker unknown. United States.

Cotton prints and solids. Back is pieced feedsack material of the same design, possibly added. Old binding was removed (holes are visible on the edges), machine stitched knife-edge added. Tied with pink cotton yarn.

$250-$400

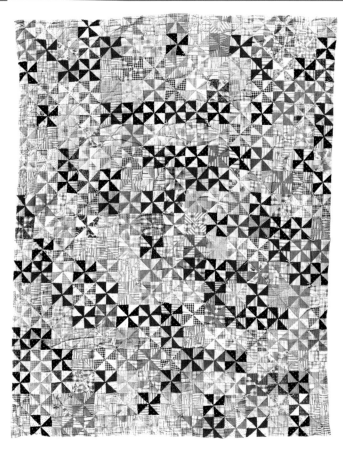

BLUE AND WHITE PINWHEELS

20th century

Maker unknown. Minnesota.

Blue and white gingham with white setting blocks; double border: blue and white. White back, blue binding. Outline quilting in pinwheel blocks, diagonal in setting blocks.

$250-$400

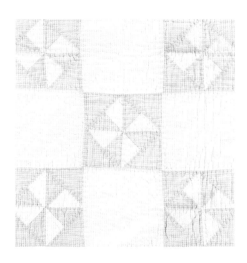

ZIGZAG BABY BLOCKS

C 1930

Maker unknown. Indiana.

Pink, blue and cream cotton solids; white, pink double border. White back, blue binding.

$100-$250

T-SQUARE VARIATION

C 1930

Maker unknown. United States.

Cotton solids and Depression-era prints. Green print back; back-to-front self-binding, possibly new.

$100-$250

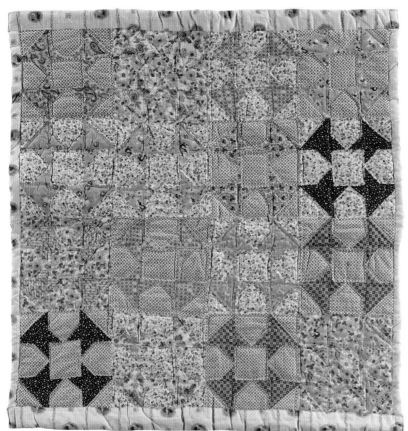

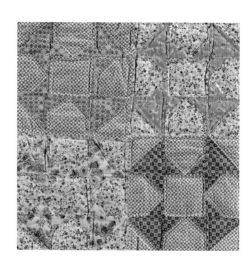

NINE-PATCH GOOSE TRACK VARIATION TOP

C 1885

Maker unknown. United States.

Cotton shirtings: plaids, stripes and checks; pink gingham sashing and outer border; inner border white cotton print; hand pieced. Purchased with extra gingham strips.

$250-$400

PINK AND WHITE BASKETS

1930s

Maker unknown. Midwestern United States.

Pink baskets and diagonal "trellis" sash, white background; applied handles. White back and binding. Diagonal hand quilting.

$100-$250

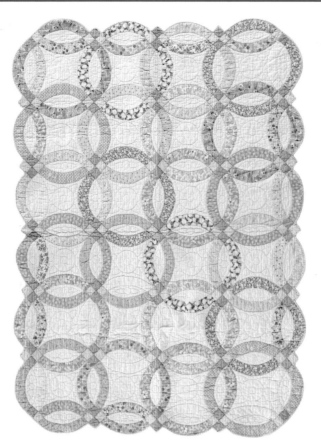

DOUBLE WEDDING RING
1930-1950
Maker unknown. United States.
Pastel cotton prints and solids. Muslin back; frayed
pink binding. Unusual design for a crib quilt.
$250-$400

SIX-POINT STARS
1930s
Maker unknown. United States.
Cotton prints on white muslin background; hand
pieced. Muslin back; prairie point binding. Hand
quilted stars and double circles.
$100-$250

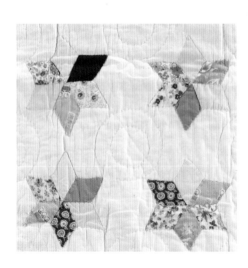

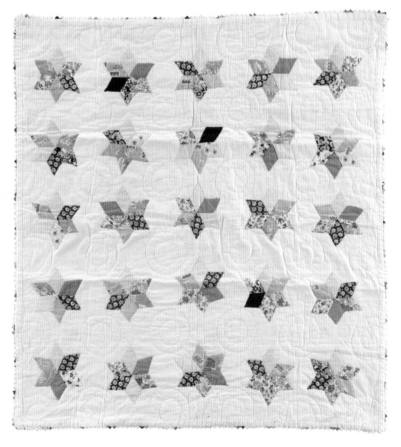

APPLIQUÉD PINEAPPLE MEDALLION

C 1840

Maker unknown. Probably United States.

Central green and yellow pineapple medallion with two buds surrounded by six borders: 1) turkey red floral print; 2) cotton print and cream triangles; 3) muslin strip with green appliqué corners; 4) cotton print and cream triangles, set opposite to #2; 5) beige floral strip with bright blue corners; and 6) turkey red print and muslin alternating squares; several documented vintage fabrics; hand pieced and appliquéd. Cream feedsack back; new red binding. Hand quilted by owner to replace poor-quality, later-addition machine quilting.

$600-$750

LONE STAR MEDALLION

1850-1875

Maker unknown. Baby quilt of the seller's great-grandfather, Minneapolis, Minnesota.

Cotton, muslin and homespun fabrics; triple border, two pieced; hand pieced. Pieced back; muslin binding.

$250-$400

SCHERENSCHNITTE PAPER CUT

Dated 1906

Signed in brown ink "For Jessica — Mabel King." Pennsylvania.

Red cotton paper-cut motif on white cotton background; red border; machine appliquéd. Cotton batting. White cotton back; front to back self-binding. Machine quilting; echo around motif; parallel lines on edges and border.

$400-$600

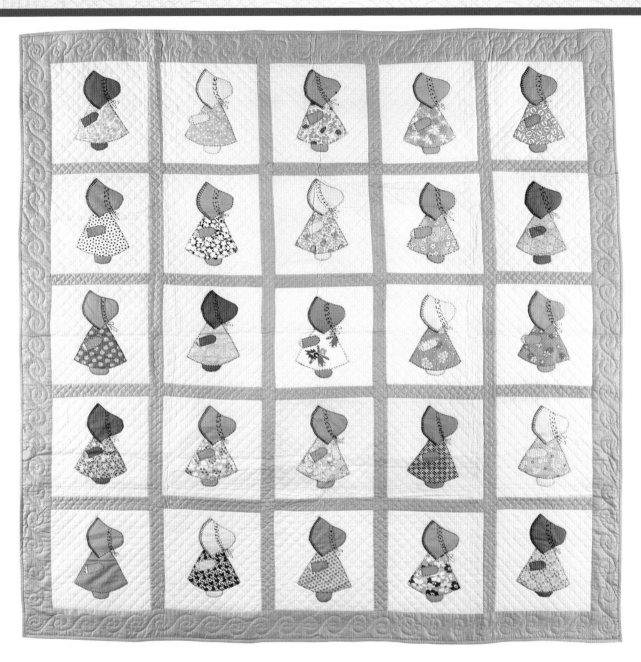

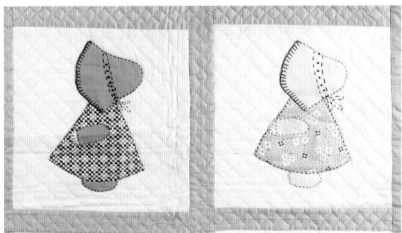

SUNBONNET SUE

C 1930

Maker unknown. United States, probably Midwest.
Cotton prints and solids on muslin background;
applied with black thread in running stitch and
buttonhole stitch; blue sashing and border. Muslin
back, knife-edge binding. Crosshatch quilting in
blocks, cable in border.

$400-$600

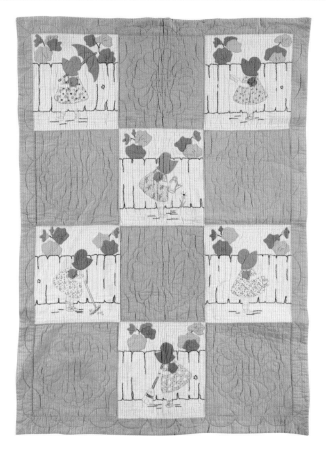

SUNBONNET GIRLS

C 1930

Maker unknown. United States, probably Midwestern.
Cotton appliqué and embroidery on white
background; pink setting blocks. Pink back; pink
mitered binding. Hand quilted: outline on figures,
sunflowers on setting blocks.

$250-$400

SUNBONNET BABIES

1920-1940

Maker unknown. Machine quilted by Diane Wiest,
Minneapolis, Minnesota.
Purchased as a top and finished by the owner. Cotton
prints and solids on muslin background. New blue
border, new back and binding.

$250-$400

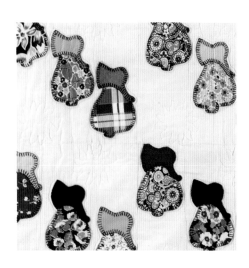

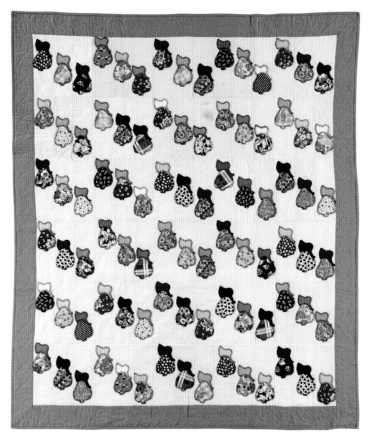

SUNBONNET SUE

Maker: La Vee Huggett, Chillicothe, Missouri.
Cotton prints and solids; blanket stitched on white background. Muslin back; pink binding, somewhat worn. Made as a gift for Vivian, the daughter of Ms. Huggett's friends R.D. and K. Jones. Vivian and her husband Al Hida named their first daughter Sue in the quilt's honor.

$400-$600

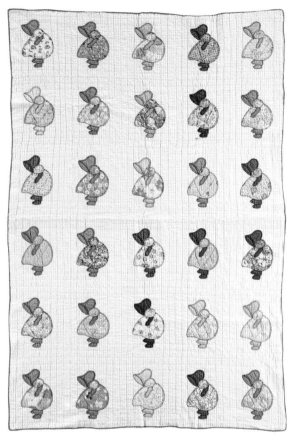

MOTHER HEN AND BABY CHICKS

1930s
Maker: mother or grandmother of the owner.
Minnesota.
Cotton appliqué on white background with embroidery; kit or pattern. Scalloped yellow border. White back and binding. Quilting follows the original pattern.

$400-$600

DAISY CHAIN

C 1930

Maker unknown. United States, probably Midwest.
Blue cotton background with four children appliquéd
at the corners of a medallion wreath of daisies; some
embroidery; very narrow white edge. Flannel batting.
White cotton back; knife-edge binding. Floral quilting
motifs. Probably a kit.

$250-$400

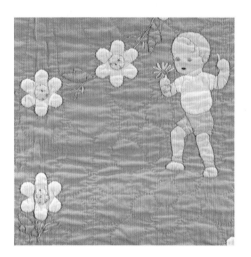

TEDDY BEARS

C 1940

Maker: Ira Hosto Zoelzer, grandmother of the owner.
Wisconsin.

Pink and blue solid cotton bears appliquéd on white
background; blanket stitch outline and embroidered
faces. Colors of bears and sashing alternate; columns
of bears face each other. Muslin back and binding.
Utility quilting.

$250-$400

PUPPY MEDALLION

1950s

Maker unknown. Made for the owner. Wisconsin. Yellow and blue cotton appliquéd on white background with embroidery. Probably a kit. Pink blanket batting. Blue cotton back; knife-edge binding. Some wear.

$250-$400

CIRCUS WAGONS

C 1950

Maker unknown. United States.

Cotton appliqués and embroidery; stamped patterns (stamped outlines around each block for embroidery or quilting are not worked); wide pink sashing. Thick cotton batting. Blue back with some piecing; blue binding. Tied with blue yarn.

$250-$400

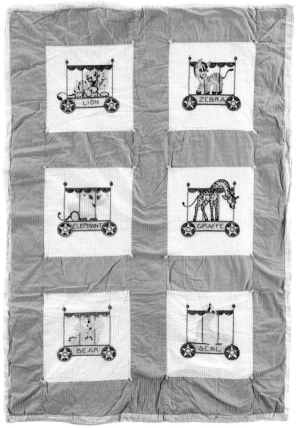

FLORAL EMBROIDERY

20th century

Maker unknown. United States.

Stamped embroidery patterns on white background; blocks joined with gold herringbone stitch; pink border. White binding.

$400-$600

EMBROIDERED NURSERY RHYMES

1950s

Maker: Glenna Martin, mother of the owner. Wisconsin.

Blocks embroidered with nursery rhyme motifs; multicolored floss; pattern by Ruby Short McKim, copyright 1935, in the Paducah Sun-Democrat. Pink sashing and outer border; white inner border. Muslin back; back-to-front self-binding. A similar blue version was made for the owner's brother.

$400-$600

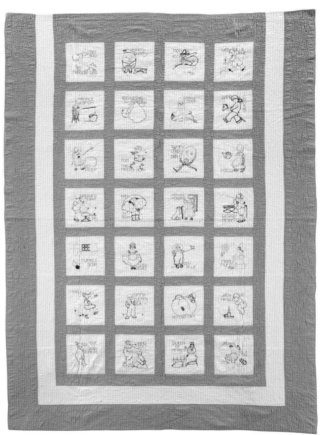

EMBROIDERED ANIMALS

C 1950

Maker: Lottie Martin, maternal grandmother of the
owner. Wisconsin.

Embroidered animal motifs on white cotton
background; multicolored floss; blue cotton sashing
with pink cotton corner squares and inner border;
blue outer border with four-patch corner squares.
Pink back; front to back self-binding. Pattern or kit.

$250-$400

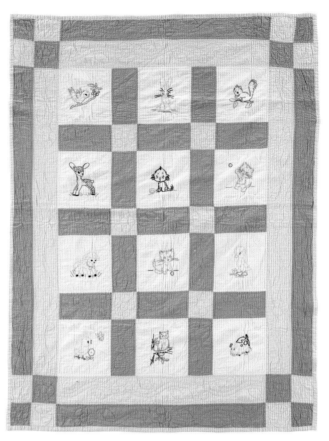

EMBROIDERED CRIB QUILT

C 1930

Maker unknown. United States.

White cotton sateen with embroidered motifs in
blue and pink floss. White cotton back; knife-edge
binding with white prairie points inserted on all
sides. Very faded.

$100-$250

BLUEBIRDS MEDALLION CRIB QUILT

Dated 1946 (top left corner)

Maker unknown. United States.

Peach acetate taffeta with birds and flowers embroidered with floss; medallion form; probably a kit. Cotton batting. Lavender acetate back; back-to-front self-binding. Hand-quilted crosshatching.

$100-$250

REDWORK CRIB QUILT

C 1910

Maker unknown. Midwestern United States.

Typical penny square motifs on white cotton background embroidered with red floss; wide red and white striped sashing and border. Muslin back; white bias binding.

$250-$400

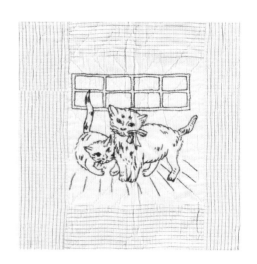

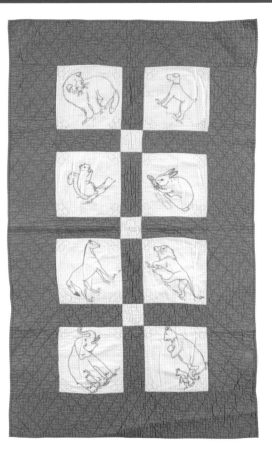

BLUEWORK ANIMALS
1930s
Maker unknown. Minnesota.
Wild and domestic animals facing each other in two rows on white background embroidered with blue floss; blue sashing with white corners; wide blue border. Blue back; back-to-front blue self-binding. Hand quilted with crosshatch.
$100-$250

BLUEWORK NURSERY RHYMES
1949
Maker Louise Vogelgestang Fuchs for her grandson Chris Fuchs. Wisconsin.
White cotton pattern squares embroidered with children's motifs in blue floss; blue and white cotton sashing and borders in an unusual configuration.
$200-$400

PRAYER CRIB QUILT

C 1955

Maker unknown. United States.

Pre-quilted kit; white cotton with cross-stitched children's figures, words, floral wreath medallion and animals; embroidery goes through all layers to the back. White satin bias binding.

$100-$250

EMBROIDERED ALPHABET

C 1975

Maker unknown. United States.

Pre-quilted kit: white cotton background cross-stitched with capital letters and children's motifs. Cotton batting. White cotton back; embroidery does not go through; new red binding applied by the owner, who also re-sized the very wide original borders.

$100-$250

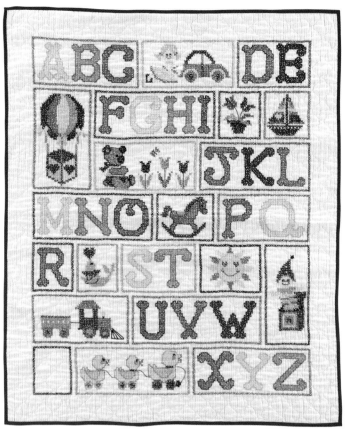

Doll Quilts

Many vintage doll quilts were made by children who were learning to sew, and their awkward stitches and uneven seams can make them endearing. Like Crib Quilts (see pages 199-220), they are most desirable if they are miniature versions of larger patterns, but the spontaneity and exuberance of many of the unpolished examples more than make up for their crudeness. Doll quilts are generally pieced, and few appliqué versions seem to exist.

At the same time as teaching youngsters sewing skills, the making of doll quilts could instill valuable lessons in color and design as well as figuring out the mathematical aspects of creating a pattern, from sizing blocks to tackling borders. Unskilled hands have obviously pieced many examples, with machine quilting found quite often, worked either by a busy mother helping a child finish a project or by a child learning to work at the sewing machine. Elaborate and finely detailed versions are most likely to have been made by an adult.

ONE-PATCH SQUARES DOLL QUILT
C 1930
Maker unknown. Midwestern United States.
Blue/turquoise print with blue-on-white polka dot print. Blue slubbed rayon backing, back-to-front self-binding.
$100 or less

ONE-PATCH SQUARES DOLL QUILT
Mid-20th century
Maker unknown. United States.
Cotton prints
$100 or less

ONE-PATCH SQUARES DOLL QUILT
C 1920
Maker unknown. United States.
Cotton prints, some indigos. Pink print back, back-to-front self-binding.
$100 or less

ONE-PATCH SQUARES DOLL QUILT

C 1945

Maker "Grandma Van," mother of the collector's childhood babysitter. Wisconsin.

Cotton scraps. Pieced back, upholstery chintz and cotton print. Knife-edge binding secured with blanket stitch. Slight damage.

$100 or less

ONE-PATCH SQUARES DOLL QUILT

C 1930

Maker unknown. United States.

Cotton print squares set in diagonal rows, prairie points border. Tied with white yarn.

$100-$250

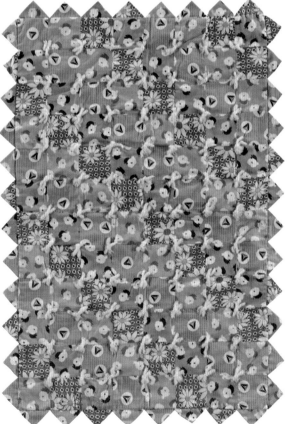

ONE-PATCH CHECKERBOARD DOLL QUILT

20th century

Maker unknown. United States.

Turquoise and white squares, cotton solids. White cotton back, back-to-front self-binding.

$100 or less

ONE-PATCH SQUARES SET ON POINT DOLL QUILT

1930-1940

Maker unknown. United States.

Hand-pieced cotton prints with solid red central cross and zigzag edge. Floral print back. Blue striped binding. Vertical machine quilting with one row of horizontal hand quilting.

$100 or less

ONE-PATCH SQUARES DOLL QUILT

1910-1925

Maker unknown. United States.

Mainly blue cotton prints set in diagonal rows alternating lights and darks. Blue back, back-to-front self-binding. Machine pieced, poor-quality hand quilting.

$100 or less

TRIP AROUND THE WORLD DOLL QUILT

C 1920

Maker unknown. United States.

Cotton prints, blue and yellow solids. Blue binding.

$100 or less

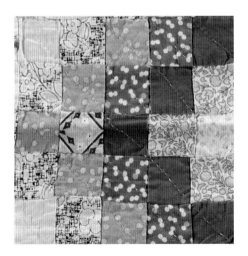

BOSTON COMMONS VARIATION DOLL QUILT

1920s

Maker unknown. United States.

Cotton squares and rectangles, solid red and white, unusual print. Print repeated on back. Knife-edge binding.

$100 or less

FOUR-PATCH STRIPPY DOLL QUILT

C 1900

Maker unknown. United States.

Cotton prints and solids in four-patch blocks, including some conversation prints; red cotton strips. Pink/green/gray cotton print back. Red binding. Tied with red yarn.

$100-$250

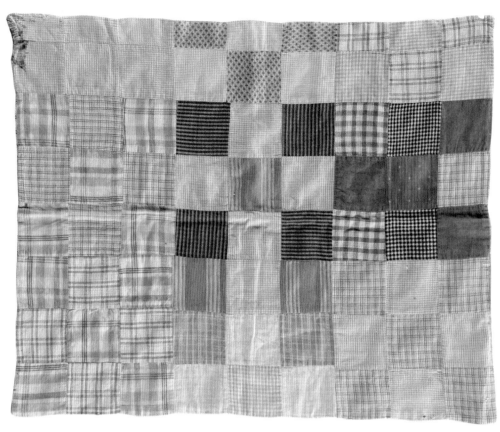

DOUBLE-SIDED NINE-PATCH DOLL QUILT

C 1900

Maker unknown. United States. Cotton checks and stripes, some solids. Mainly shirtings. 3 X 5 rows of nine-patch blocks have been folded to make the quilt 3 X 2.5 rows. Knife-edge binding, no batting.

$100 or less

NINE-PATCH CHAIN DOLL QUILT

1900s

Maker unknown. United States.

Cotton indigos and shirtings with muslin. Muslin back. Pieced blue binding. Hand quilting.

$100-$250

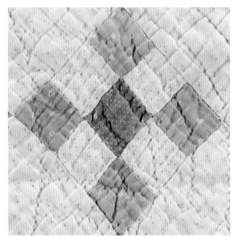

OHIO STAR FOUR-BLOCK DOLL QUILT

C 1890

Maker unknown. United States.

Cotton shirting Ohio Star blocks set on point with brown print spacers. Brown print back. Brown striped binding. Some wear front and back.

$100-$250

NINE-PATCH SQUARE IN A SQUARE DOLL QUILT

20th century

Maker unknown. United States.

Hand-pieced cotton solid centers, print outer squares, brown solid sashing and border. Knife-edge binding. Outline quilting.

$100 or less

COURTHOUSE STEPS DOLL QUILT

20th century

Maker unknown. United States.

Cotton print with red centers, set light-and-dark.

Black print binding.

$100-$250

TUMBLERS DOLL QUILT

C 1930

Maker unknown. United States.

Machine-pieced cotton solids. Pink cotton back.

Knife-edge binding, one edge unfinished. No quilting.

$100 or less

RED AND WHITE CHEVRON DOLL QUILT
20th century
Maker unknown. United States.
Red/pink striped and blue on white polka dot
cottons. Blue and white backing. Wide back-to-front
binding.
$100-$250

CRAZY FOUR-PATCH DOLL QUILT
1920-1940
Maker unknown. United States.
Blue and red cotton prints. Blue striped back. Red
binding.
$100 or less

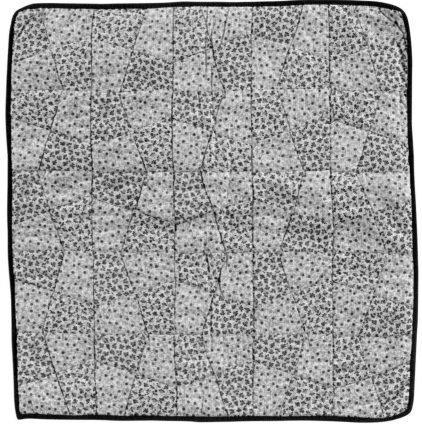

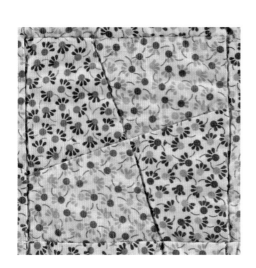

CONTAINED CRAZY DOLL QUILT

C 1945
Maker unknown. United States.
Silks, velvets, brocades, satins and cottons on foundation fabric. High-quality hand embroidered feather stitching in pink perle cotton thread, which acts as quilting. Knife-edge binding. No batting.
$400-$600

YO-YO DOLL QUILT

20th century
Maker unknown. United States.
Cotton prints set in Trip-Around-the-World configuration.
$100-$250

GRANDMOTHER'S FLOWER GARDEN DOLL QUILT

1930s

Maker unknown. United States.

Cotton print rings, muslin paths and centers.
Hexagons 1". Blue/white gingham check back. Knife-
edge binding. Outline quilting.

$100-$250

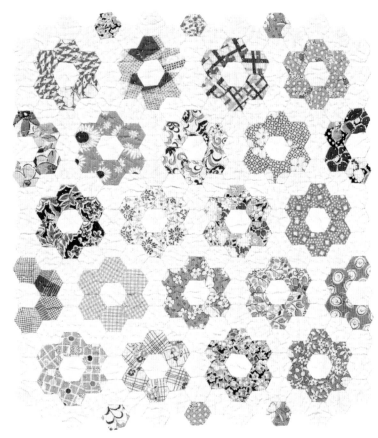

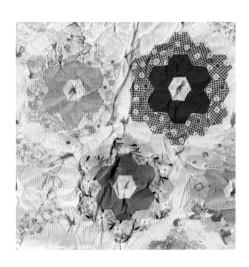

GRANDMOTHER'S FLOWER GARDEN DOLL QUILT

20th century

Maker unknown. United States.

Miniature bright cotton hexagons. Muslin back; knife-
edge binding.

$100 or less

CHAPTER 6

NON-TRADITIONAL QUILTS

African American Quilts

Until recently, collectors largely ignored quilts made by African Americans, particularly those made in the improvisational style. There are of course exquisitely made quilts that have been documented as having been made by slaves, but they were not used by the makers and have been passed down not through the black families but by those of the white slave owners. Most of the examples with such provenance are in museums, though some are in the hands of private collectors, and it is probable that some quilts from the first half of the 19th century were made by African American slaves who will never get credit.

The popularity of exhibits like The Quilts of Gee's Bend and the scholarly research being done on improvisational quilts, coupled with the romantic idea of the Underground Railroad and the rise of Black Studies programs have contributed to the attention belatedly being paid to this area. Many "traditional" quilters decry the improvisational aesthetic of these quilts—the lack of squared-off corners, the often jarring use of color, the utility quilting—but the genre has become a popular area for collectors and prices have risen to reflect this shift.

Collectors should avoid a number of pitfalls. Most vintage African American quilts have little or no provenance, but this is true of the vast majority of older quilts. The style and the workmanship can provide clues to African American origins. The idea that African American quiltmakers have used patterns found in African textiles in an innate way is perhaps stretching a point, though it is true that the strip format is widespread in both.

The story of quilts being used as message boards for slaves escaping along the Underground Railroad routes is being questioned widely (and any quilt offered as having been such a signal should be viewed with great suspicion).

Note: Some of the quilts in this section are later than the general cutoff date in this book, but the sudden popularity of the genre and the scarcity of such quilts, as well as the enormous difficulty in dating them, has led me to open up the criterion for this category, and its unique characteristics have influenced my decision to make this a separate section from the general patchwork chapter.

In this chapter
235 African American
248 Siddi

LAZY GAL STRIP QUILT
Post 1950
Maker unknown. Texas.
Red and white solid cotton strips. Muslin backing,
back-to-front self-binding.
$250-$400

DENIM STRIP QUILT
20th century
Maker unknown. United States.
Denim strips, one with an original jeans patch and
one with pocket outline. Blanket batting. Muslin back,
back-to-front self-binding. Tied with red string.
$400-$600

RECTANGULAR STRIPPY

20th century

Maker unknown. United States.

Cotton print rectangles. Check cotton cheater cloth.
Back pieced from matching fabrics. Back-to-front
binding.

$250-$400

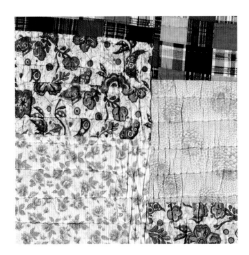

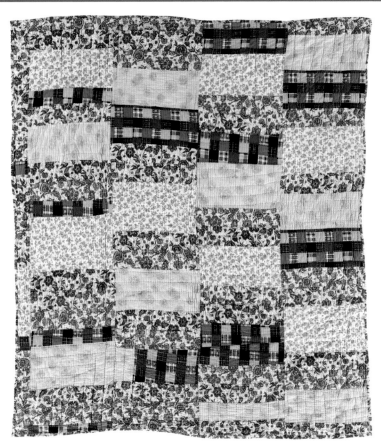

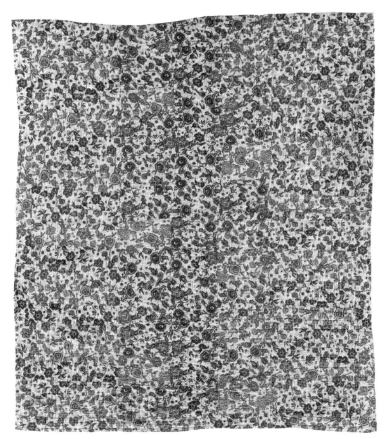

DOUBLE-SIDED HOUSETOP

1930-1945

Maker unknown. Alabama.

Top: denim and cotton stripes and solids. Back: cotton prints, stripes and plaids. Back-to-front self-binding.

$600-$750

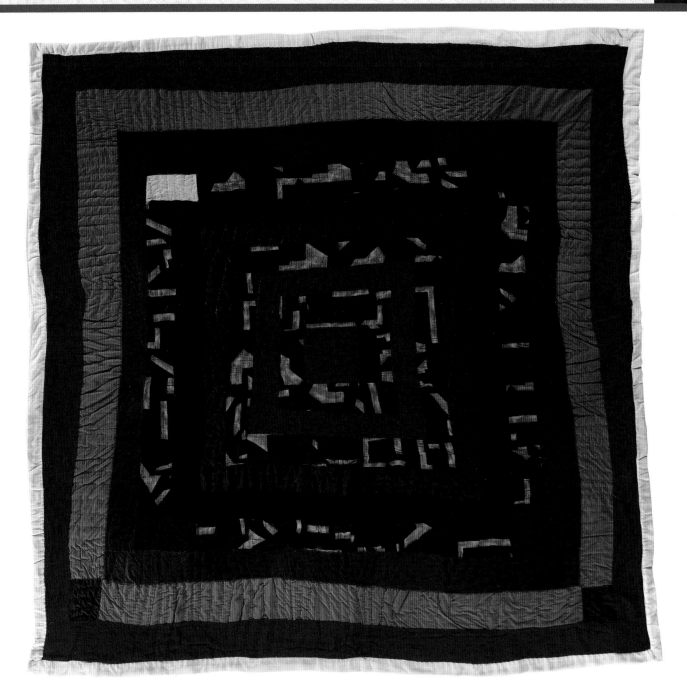

CABIN IN THE COTTON HOUSETOP

C 2000

Maker: Annie B. Pettway. Gee's Bend, Alabama.
Cotton knits, velour and plain weaves. Muslin back,
back-to-front self-binding. Utility quilting.

$1,000-$1,500

DENIM HOUSETOP

2004

Maker Lucy Mingo. Gee's Bend, Alabama.
Denim strips, graded colors. Green cotton backing,
back-to-front self-binding. Utilitarian quilting.

More than $5,000

COURTHOUSE STEPS

C 1970

Maker: Mary Maxtion. Boligee, Alabama.
Cotton strips. Gray cotton plaid sashing; black inner,
red outer borders. Cotton sailboat print backing,
back-to-front self-binding.

$600-$750

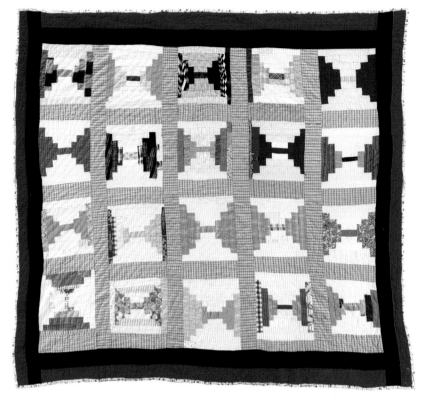

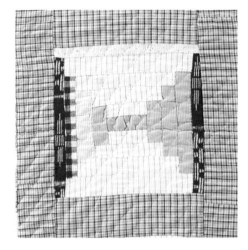

CHECKERBOARD ABSTRACT

C 1900

Maker: probably Gladys Fry. Tennessee hill country.
Wool, denim and homespun, mainly plaids, stripes
and solids. Blanket batting. Brown/beige print
backing, back-to-front binding. Tied to the back with
brown string.

$750-$1,000

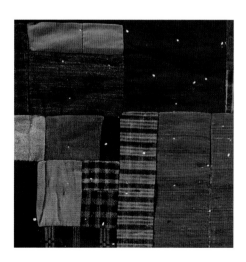

CHECKERBOARD

C 1900
Maker unknown. Tennessee hill country.
Wool, denim and homespun plaids, stripes, and
solids. Greige homespun back, back-to-front self-
binding.

$400-$600

IMPROVISATIONAL CRAZY QUILT

Pre-1930
Maker unknown. Northern Arkansas.
Wool solid scraps. Thin, faded paisley back, one end
pieced. Knife-edge binding. Tied with red string.

$400-$600

"X" QUILT

Post 1950

Maker unknown. Eastern Texas.

Cotton solids and prints. Blue backing, back-to-front self-binding. Curved quilting.

$250-$400

8-POINT STAR VARIATION

C 1970

Maker: Mary Maxtion. Boligee, Alabama.

Bright cotton colors and prints; dark green sash with print corners; bright green border on three sides, orange checked border on fourth side; yellow end border, cotton print border top and bottom. Pieced print back; back-to-front self-binding.

$600-$750

ESCAPING STARS

C 1930

Maker unknown. Green Castle, Missouri. Wool suiting, solids. Striped wool back, back-to-front self-binding. Tied with green string.

$600-$750

PINWHEEL VARIATION

C 1960

Maker: Melissa Pettway. Gee's Bend, Alabama. Yellow and blue scraps, various fabrics. Cotton batting. Muslin back and binding. Some damage.

$1,500-$2,000

JACOB'S LADDER

Post 1950

Maker unknown. East Texas.

Cotton solids, prints, checks. Muslin back. Front-to-back binding.

$400-$600

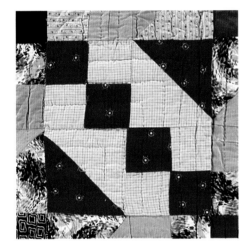

HOURGLASS AND CHAIN

Post 1950

Maker unknown. South Georgia.

Cotton solids, wide cotton print border. Pieced back, some staining, back-to-front wide floral binding, some fading.

$400-$600

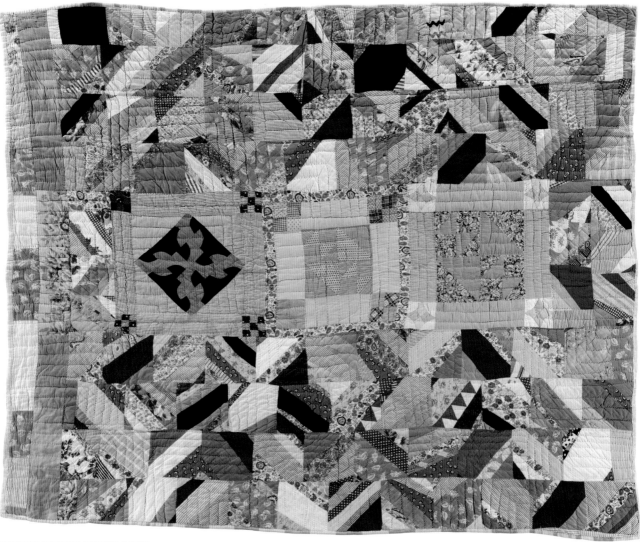

THREE-BLOCK MEDALLION

C 1930

Maker unknown. Georgetown, Texas.

Cotton prints, seersucker and feedsacks. Four rows of string-pieced blocks act as borders to three central blocks: one Drunkard's Path and two Fox and Geese; each with sashes and pieced corner squares. Striped flannel back. Straight-line quilting.

$600-$750

A VARIETY OF PATTERNS

1994

Maker Edward Harris. Quilter Freddie Johnson.
Tutwiler, Mississippi.

Cotton prints and solids. Navy back and binding.
Thick polyester batting.

$750-$1,000

TEXAS CHURCH SIGNATURE QUILT

C 1950

Makers unknown. Made for the Mission Home
Church of the World. Central Texas.

Blue and white album blocks. Names and addresses
embroidered in red. Many addresses are PO Boxes, in
towns including Altair, Columbus, Garwood, Houston,
San Antonio and Wharton. Brown print back, back-to-
front binding.

$600-$750

Siddi Quilts

With the surge of interest in African American quilts has come a rise in interest in quilts made in other ethnicities. One such area that bears watching is a little-known group of quiltmakers in the state of Karnataka on the west coast of India. Known as Siddi, they are descendants of Africans enslaved and brought to the region by the Portuguese who settled Goa beginning in the 16th century.

These groups gradually moved southward and settled in the Western Ghatt mountains, where they created remote diapora communities that still exist today and number about 20,000. While they are part of the Indian culture in many ways, they retain some traditions from their African heritage, including the making of unique patchwork quilts called **kawandi**.

The quilts in this section were all made in this century, but many of them contain vintage fabrics not seen in the West, and their highly collectible qualities led to my decision to include them.

Most are made to be used within the family, but in 2004 the Siddi Women's Quilting Cooperative was set up to encourage skilled makers to create masterpieces to provide needed income in one of the poorest areas of the Third World, with all profits from sales going back to the Coop.

Unlike most western quilts, a kawandi begins at one corner. The backing is a layer of cotton saris, and patches or strips are added around the quilt with a running backstitch, creating a highly textured product. Some of the kawandi have no embellishment outside the tassels of yarn that always decorate the corners of the quilt, but many are decorated with **tikeli**, small bright fabric scraps that sparkle like jewels on the surface.

Central areas often contain patches that function like center medallions, and corners often contain squares made from folded patches that create a mitered effect called a **phula**, or flower.

To find out more about Siddi quilts and the cooperative venture, contact Henry Drewal at hjdrewal@wisc.edu.

KAWANDI CRIB QUILT

C 2000

Maker Shanta Mingel. Mainalli, Karnataka, India.
Multicolored fabric scraps set in frame format, white outer border; red phula at each corner.

$400-$600

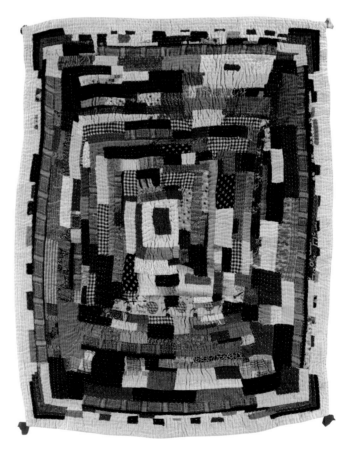

KAWANDI CRIB QUILT

C 2000

Maker Fatima Imamsahib. Gunjavati, Karnataka, India.
Multicolored fabric scraps, predominantly white and
red, set in frame format with red and white pieced
border and blue binding; red phula at each corner;
label on front.

$400-$600

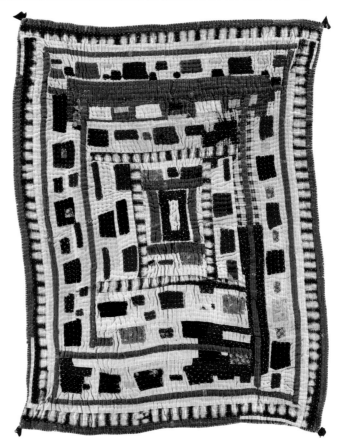

KAWANDI SMALL QUILT

C 2000

Maker Bibijan Adkesur. Mainalli, Karnataka, India.
Multicolored fabric strips set in frame format; red
phula at each corner.

$400-$600

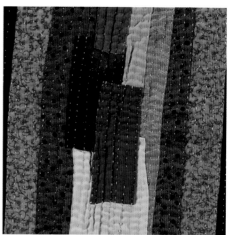

KAWANDI CRIB QUILT
C 2000

Maker Rosa Simau. Mainalli, Karnataka, India.
Multicolored fabric strips set in frame format, several frames are a single color; brown phula at each corner.
$400-$600

KAWANDI SMALL QUILT
C 2000

Maker Bibijan Ibrahimsahib. Kendalgiri, Karnataka, India.
Multicolored fabric scraps and strips; dark center set in frame format, light sides with bright-colored mitered ribbon strips in each corner; blue and yellow phula at corners and along sides.
$400-$600

KAWANDI SMALL QUILT

C 2000

Maker Mabobi Hassansahib Bhagwathi. Kendalgiri, Karnataka, India.

Multicolored fabric scraps and strips; abstract red center with numerous narrow frames, some pieced in repeating patterns; many tikeli; mitered bright-colored ribbon strips in each corner; blue and green phula at each corner.

$400-$600

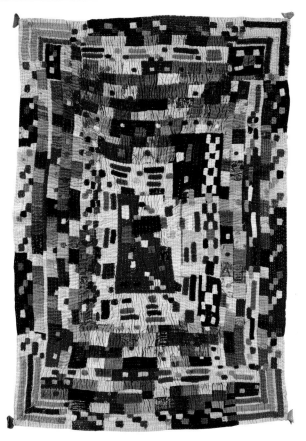

KAWANDI SMALL QUILT

C 2000

Maker Anjeline Ganapati. Mainalli, Karnataka, India.

Multicolored fabric strips and scraps set in frame format; wide randomly pieced binding; red and white phula in each corner.

$400-$600

KAWANDI CRIB QUILT

C 2000

Maker Rabia Bakarsahib. Gunjavati, Karnataka, India.
Multicolored fabric squares and mainly white strips;
pink squares outlined on two sides with mitered
green, gold and rose-red ribbon strips in each corner.
Green and blue outer border/binding; blue wool
phula in each corner.

$400-$600

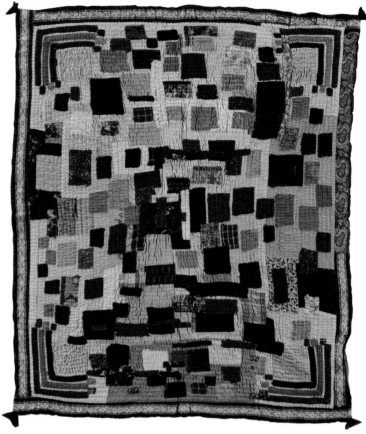

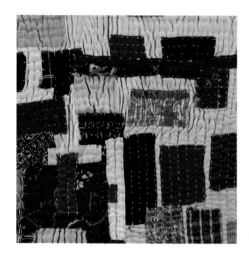

KAWANDI SMALL QUILT

C 2000

Maker Ramijabi Madarsahib. Kendalgiri, Karnataka,
India.
Multicolored fabric squares and rectangles arranged
in a random checkerboard; some tikeli; mitered
multicolored ribbon strips form the corners; pink and
green phula in the corners.

$400-$600

KAWANDI CRIB QUILT

C 2000

Maker unknown. Probably Kendalgiri, Karnataka, India. Multicolored fabric squares and rectangles in a random arrangement with tikeli in contrasting colors as surface decoration; mitered multicolored ribbon strips in each corner; brown phula, three in each corner.

$400-$600

KAWANDI SMALL QUILT

C 2000

Maker Rosa Simau. Mainalli, Karnataka, India. Multicolored fabric strips arranged in long frame format; mainly solids with some prints; red phula in each corner.

$400-$600

KAWANDI LARGE QUILT

C 2000

Maker Mary Mariani. Mainalli, Karnataka, India. Multicolored fabric strips set around a red center square in frame format; pieced binding; red phula in the corners. Double bed size.

$750-$1,000

KAWANDI LARGE QUILT

C 2000

Maker Sushila Ruzai. Mainalli, Karnataka, India. Multicolored fabric strips and rectangles; diagonal rows of multicolored squares; pieced binding; one phula at each corner. Twin bed size.

$750-$1,000

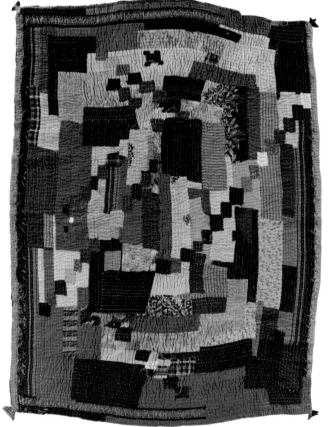

KAWANDI LARGE QUILT

C 2000

Maker Khatumbi Muzavar. Mainalli, Karnataka, India.
Narrow multicolored fabric strips set in frame format;
highly intricate design; one phula at each corner.
Double bed size.

$750-$1,000

KAWANDI LARGE QUILT

C 2000

Maker Flora Introse. Mainalli, Karnataka, India.
Multicolored fabric strips set in frame format around
a bright pink center; a few tikeli. King bed size.

$750-$1,000

Duplicate Rich Historical Stitches

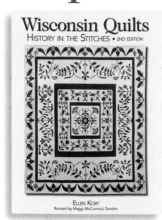

by Ellen Kort

Wisconsin Quilts: History in the Stitches brings readers 100 antique quilts stitched by immigrants between the 1800s and the mid-20th century, through times of war, economic development and depression, with continued perseverance. Readers learn to create 10+ quilt blocks.
Softcover • 8-¼ x 10-⅞ • 208 pages
50 color photos
Item# Z1481 • $34.99

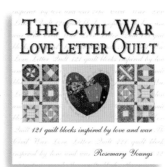

by Rosemary Youngs

Get wrapped up in the loves and lives of 11 Civil War soldiers and the beautiful quilts their stories inspired. Using 121 different blocks, you can create 14 projecst, including a full-size quilt, lap quilts, wall hangings and table runners.
Softcover • 8 x 8 • 288 pages
20 color photos, 300 color illus.
Item# Z0751 • $24.99

by Kim Deneault

Discover a stress-free new appliqué technique in the detailed instructions and 175 color photos and illustrations of this book. Plus, you'll find 12+ designs for small, quick projects, as well as more complex projects, featured on a pattern insert.
Softcover • 8-¼ x 10-⅞ • 128 pages
25 b&w illus. • 175 color photos
Item# Z0765 • $24.99

by Darlene Zimmerman

This 12-project book delivers beautiful quilts, perfect for each month of the year, while drawing readers into the beauty and bounty of life at fictional Lavender Hill Farm.
Softcover • 8-¼ x 10-⅞8 • 128 pages
65 color photos and 132 illustrations
Item# Z0380 • $22.99

by Glenna Hailey

A comprehensive overview of feed sacks produced from 1930-1960 and 12 modern designs for coordinating projects, from bed quilts to wall hangings, using fat quarters/eighths of original or reproduction fabrics.
Softcover • 8-¼ x 10-⅞ • 112 pages
75 color photos
Item# Z0850 • $22.99

by Elaine Waldschmitt

Create perfect curves every time with this simple technique. Once you've mastered the technique, you can create any of the 12 featured projects. **Bonus CD with 20 appliqué templates included.**
Softcover • 8-¼ x 10-⅞ • 128 pages
200 color photos
Item# Z1659 • $24.99

Order directly from the publisher at www.krausebooks.com

Krause Publications, Offer **ACB8**
P.O. Box 5009
Iola, WI 54945-5009
www.krausebooks.com

Call **800-258-0929** 8 a.m. - 5 p.m. to order direct from the publisher, or visit booksellers nationwide or antiques and hobby shops.

Please reference offer **ACB8** with all direct-to-publisher orders

Connect. Create. Explore at www.mycraftivity.com